For Jodie —

June 2023

THE FATHOMLESS TIDES OF THE HEART

Sending love + all blessings

love

Caroleyn

Also by Peter Thabit Jones

Poetry

Tacky Brow (Outposts Publications, UK, 1974)

The Apprenticeship (Cwm Nedd Press, UK, 1977)

Clocks Tick Differently (Celtion Poetry Series, UK, 1980)

Visitors (Poetry Wales Press, UK, 1986)

The Cold Cold Corner (Dark Lane Poetry, UK, 1995)

Ballad of Kilvey Hill (Swansea Bay Publishers/Eastside Poetry, UK, 1999)

The Lizard Catchers (Cross-Cultural Communications, USA, 2006/reprinted 2007 & 2008)

POET TO POET #1: Bridging the Waters: Swansea to Sag Harbor,
with American poet Vince Clemente (Cross-Cultural Communications, USA, and The Seventh Quarry Press, UK, 2008)

Whispers of the Soul, with American poet Vince Clemente
(a bilingual collection: English/Romanian). Translated by Dr. Olimpia Iacob (Editura Fundatiei Poezia Iasi, Romania, 2008)

Poems from a Cabin on Big Sur (Cross-Cultural Communications, USA, 2011)

Where the Butterflies Go/Songs for a Dark Bird (Two bilingual collections of poems in one book. Romania's Aura Cristi's *Where the Butterflies Go*/Peter's *Songs for a Dark Bird*. Translated by Dr. Olimpia Iacob and Jim Kacian (Timpul Publishing, Romania, 2014)

Selected Poems (bilingual collection: English/Romanian). Translated by Dr. Monica Manolachi of the University of Bucharest. (Bibliotecha Universalis/ Collectiile Revistei 'Orizont Literar Contemporan', 2016)

Garden of Clouds/New and Selected Poems (Cross-Cultural Communications, USA, 2020)

A Cancer Notebook (Cross-Cultural Communications, USA, and The Seventh Quarry Press, UK, 2022)

Prose

Dylan Thomas Walking Tour of Greenwich Village, New York, with Aeronwy
Thomas (for the Wales International Centre, New York/Welsh Assembly
Government, 2008, PDF www.walesworldnation.com)
PODCAST: www.dylanthomaswalkingtourmp3.com
Dylan Thomas Walking Tour of Greenwich Village, New York tourist pocket book,
with Aeronwy Thomas (Cross-Cultural Communications, USA, and The Seventh
Quarry Press, UK, 2014)
Dylan Thomas Walking Tour of Greenwich Village, New York smartphone app, with
Aeronwy Thomas (DT100/Dylan Thomas Centenary, Welsh Government, Literature
Wales, and The British Council, 2014)
America, Aeronwy, and Me/Dylan Thomas Tribute Tour (Cross-Cultural
Communications, USA, and The Seventh Quarry Press, UK, 2019)
America, Aeronwy, and Me/Dylan Thomas Tribute Tour (Cross-Cultural
Communications, USA, and The Seventh Quarry Press, UK, 2019)
Remembering Vince Clemente/Editor (The Seventh Quarry Press, UK, 2021)

Drama

The Boy and the Lion's Head/A Verse Drama (bilingual: English/Romanian).
Translated by Dr. Olimpia Iacob (Citadela Publishing, Romania, 2009)
The Fire in the Wood/A Prose and Verse Drama, (Cross-Cultural Communications,
USA, and The Seventh Quarry Press, UK, 2017)
The Boy and the Lion's Head/A Verse Drama (New Feral Press, USA, 2017)
Under the Raging Moon/A Drama in Four Acts (Cross-Cultural Communications,
USA, and The Seventh Quarry Press, UK, 2022)

DVDs

Walking with Dylan Thomas/documentary film based on the *Dylan Thomas Walking
Tour of Greenwich Village* (Cross-Cultural Communications, USA, and The Seventh
Quarry Press, UK, 2010)
The Poet, the Hunchback, and the Boy/drama (Dylan Thomas Theatre, Holly Tree
Productions, and The Seventh Quarry Press, 2014)

THE FATHOMLESS TIDES OF THE HEART

Carolyn Mary Kleefeld

American Poet And Artist

a biography
by
Peter Thabit Jones

Cross-Cultural Communications
New York, USA

The Seventh Quarry Press,
Swansea, Wales, UK
2023

Cross-Cultural Communications
239 Wynsum Avenue
Merrick, New York 11566-4725 USA
Tel: (516) 868-5635 / Fax: (516) 379-1901
cccpoetry@aol.com

The Seventh Quarry Press
8 Cherry Crescent
Swansea SA4 9FG Wales, UK
Tel: (UK) 01792449161
seventhquarry@btinternet.com
www.seventhquarrypress.com

Library of Congress Control Number: 2023931293
ISBN 978-0-89304-691-0
UK ISBN 978-1-9196100-4-7

Cover photo of Carolyn Kleefeld by Dennis Wyszynski
Cover photo of Big Sur Coast by Tiger Windwalker

First Edition
Printed in the US

To Carolyn

And to the dear friends I have made in Big Sur and Carmel during my annual writer-in-residence summer breaks in Carolyn's cabin, The Rainbow Room, over the past ten years.

Author's Note:

When I am writing, I use UK English. When I am quoting from Carolyn's writings, I use American English.

Additional Acclaim for *The Fathomless Tides of the Heart*

"Peter Thabit Jones documents throughout his compelling biography this fascinating portrait of a woman who was born into privilege and shunned its trappings to seek a more difficult road of spiritual fulfillment. To the amazement of others, she rejected the overtures of Hollywood and turned to poetry, art, and personal growth. During her journey she meets great thinkers and artists who prove to be influential and inspire her to keep searching. Now a very accomplished poet and artist, possibly even more important to her is the spiritual peace she has found. Peter has created an engrossing and delightful read!"

Larry Levy
Author of *The Mary Handley Mystery Series*

"Peter Thabit Jones has created a beautifully constructed biography of Carolyn, whose heart of love she shares through her gifts of poetry and art, nourishing our souls, awakening them from sleep. Through Peter's words and his inclusion of many journal entries by Carolyn throughout her life, we are able to glimpse the rarest of humans, a highly conscious being who embraces solitude, a nourishing break from the voices of pollution demanding to be heard, and a teacher of finding peace, letting go of what doesn't harness our inner joy. Through her appreciation of Mother Earth and all living things, we are reminded to open our eyes and give thanks for all creation."

Marcelene Dyer
Widow of Dr. Wayne W. Dyer, birth mother of their 7 children, abiding spiritual presence

In "The Fathomless Tides of the Heart," we read about Carolyn's past, her childhood, family, storytelling, teenage adventures (!), psychology, friendships, creativity, sex, art, culture, and much more. It's as if the author, Peter Thabit Jones, is writing in front of a crystal ball. Page by page the picture emerges, of an inner world which is creatively expressed in a multitude of ways. Through the decades, Carolyn's voice, curious and thankful, runs like a common thread: always engaging the reader, always in step with the passage of time. We can be thankful to Peter Thabit Jones for writing this compelling portrait.

Magnus Torén
Executive Director, Henry Miller Library

Contents

Carolyn Mary Kleefeld, American poet and artist
© Carolyn Mary Kleefeld Collection

Foreword

It is 5th September, 2016, and I am in McGowan House in Monterey, California. I have travelled in from Big Sur with Carolyn Mary Kleefeld, international American poet and artist and a leading figure on the literary and art scenes. The *Monterey County Weekly* has correctly described her as a "Big Sur icon". I am a writer-in-residence (my seventh summer) for two months in Carolyn's cabin, called The Rainbow Room, in Big Sur. I am an invited participant at the literary event that is taking place in McGowan House, organized by American writer and sculptor John Dotson, who lives in Carmel.

Among the pre-event wine drinking and food nibbling, the chatting between participants and audience members, Carolyn is sitting on a chair and drawing on a pad with a black-Sharpie pen. Lines become shapes and shapes become shapes within a shape. For a moment, I see the young Carolyn in the adult Carolyn, the need to draw or write, or both, as she did as a talented young girl, when she produced her first wonderfully original and illustrated book *The Nanose in Nanoseland*, aged nine-years-old. I see her need to still lose herself in the physical act of exploring her imagination, even in the company of others, isolate herself from her surroundings, to go into the depths of herself in a sacred way.

She says she answers to an inner necessity to create, that there is no discipline, no will power, she just "shows up". She feels we swim towards our nourishment and would say that creating is her nourishment. Anyone who gets to know Carolyn, who becomes a friend, will experience her primal need to always have a pad and coloured pens handy, be it in a car, on a plane, in a restaurant, or at home. These pads, like a poet's personal notebook of observations and jottings for potential poems, often contain the seeds for more substantial works of art. Van Gogh, Picasso, and all the other great painters, had their working pads.

She resolutely protects her freedom to write and paint, a living endorsement of her sculptor friend Edmund Kara's statement, "The less distraction, the more intense the focus". She has been called 'the Garbo of the central coast'. She comments on her life in one of her journal entries, "Being a nocturnal animal, I live a half-life. From noon on is enough for me of the purposeful energies, although I live (usually) in the Zen of the effortless, in meditation, contemplation. Alan Watts lectured about this wondrous other way, the Taoist way, which is so right for me, so opposite from the world's way. Perhaps the world's way is left-brained and literal, along with its fierce will to succeed. I never liked that style of living. That's why school and university were prisons to me." A born iconoclast, Carolyn has never felt at ease within and with the established systems, be it school, college, or the art world.

I have had the privilege, for this book, of reading Carolyn's many journal writing manuscripts, written over a thirty-year period, some as thick as a bible; and her dedication to the written word, the awareness, as poet Seamus Heaney said, that "Words are doors themselves", is truly remarkable and admirable.

Carolyn, in fact, has carried out her journal writing since childhood. In her journals, she unfolds her thoughts in a stream of consciousness way, in an organic manner. It is an unabashed releasing of emotions, ideas, statements, philosophies, questions, fragmented themes, long and short paragraphs of prose, startling poetic lines and phrases. She allows no boundaries in her thoughts and a beautiful paragraph of nature observations can leap into bristling observations about the materialism of modern life and the madness of the warmongers. Reading the journal entries, one is aware of an intelligent mind sieving aspects of a variety of subjects for the gold nuggets of her creative vision. She often makes use of the five senses and one recalls the statement by William Blake that the five senses are " the chief inlets of Soul in this Age".

To stand in front of an unfinished painting on one of her easels (she sometimes works on two paintings at a time) in the painting area of the large living room in her Big Sur home, one feels the same committed energy, the same defiant need for an unbridled individuality and originality.

Her writings and her paintings come from the same source, a deep well of curiosity about the known and the unknown, the light and the dark of being alive. The fact that the window of her painting area looks out on the Pacific Ocean is appropriate as she, like the ever-working sea, to paraphrase Dylan Thomas, is "singing in her chains".

She once said in an interview, "Painting speaks to me in a manner that is pre-lingual, expressing my primal nature, reflecting through poetic symbolism what C.G. Jung referred to as "the language of 1,000 tongues." Through the medium of words, sounds, and rhythms, my writing impels an integrative weaving, while my painting translates deeper impressions into light, color, and shape. However, both my writing and painting are lyrical in nature and share a symbolic language.

My art and writing seem to have their own autonomous lives; yet sometimes they serendipitously express the same theme, which I'm not usually aware of until later. So both art forms dance in a complementary duet in their own time. Whether painting or writing, I embark upon a spontaneous journey on the crest of the Tao's wave, an exploration born of passion, spawned by the Mystery. I am continually amazed by what manifests on the page or canvas, and often have found that my artwork precedes my life-experience, foreseeing the future."

To have a one-to-one conversation with Carolyn is to also experience the same energy that unleashes her writings and paintings. One is warmed by the passion in her comments, whether formed down the years or freshly thought throwaway lines, on an array of subjects; and she can shoot down a too-serious truism with a quick blast of well-timed laughter.

Carolyn is a long-time admirer of certain writers, such as William Blake, Jalāl ad-Dīn Muhammad Rūmī, Rainer Maria Rilke, Nikos Kazantzakis, Baruch Spinoza, Herman Hesse, D. H. Lawrence, Fyodor Dostoyevsky, Benjamin De Casseres, Anaïs Nin, Aldous and Laura Huxley, Albert Camus, and Dylan Thomas. She prefers writers from the last century, established literary greats, those working in a period when life was slower, less complex and technological. She likes to go into their worlds and travel on journeys with those minds that brought books that changed the weather of literature for the better with their visionary light.

Sometimes when walking up the slight incline of path through her beautiful forested garden, inhabited by statues, such as deer and a Buddha, with the ocean on one's left side lap-lapping its wide rhythms through the day, one hears a loud storm of amplified music as opposed to the usual monastery-like silence. As one gets closer and enters the back entrance of her home, one can be audio-entertained by Leonard Cohen, Roy Orbison, John Lennon, Celine Dion, and Sarah Brightman, or a selection of classical music, such as Mozart, Beethoven, Tchaikovsky, Chopin, and Andrea Bocelli, depending on her choice. She often plays music whilst painting. Carolyn has said, "When I paint I'm always in movement, I'm in synchrony with the music I play." She also likes to paint in silence.

The once childhood prima ballerina likes to wear dance shoes whilst painting as the rhythms of the music colour the moods of her creativity. It was music that drove the young Carolyn to dance and that is why she took up ballet. She was invited when very young to join the Bolshoi International Ballet.

Much of her journal writing is done in the early evening in her swimming pool, which has a breathtaking view of the ocean when not haunted by an overwhelming ghost of a fog. In between swimming laps, she will fill the blank pages of a journal with writings that may eventually mature into aphorisms, poems, prose-pieces, short stories, and substantial works. She will stay in the pool until evening submits to the night's darkness and the smoke of the fog thickens and plays with the beginning of a thinly iced chilly wind, or on a clear night, a full moon places a broad milky path of light across the gently trembling glass of the Pacific.

One sometimes hears her sing a snatch of a happy song, or one hears a scattering of her laughter during a phone call. Sometimes there is an echoing call to Needja, her and John the late property manager's beloved adopted cat. John W. Larson, in fact, started working for Carolyn in 1986 and she always referred to him as her closest friend, her 'Noah of the Ark', until his untimely death in March 2018. Without John's innate practicality, Carolyn would never have survived on the secluded and, at times, perilous mountain cliffs. She is also very fortunate in having Laura Zabrowski as her Personal Assistant. Laura, who resides in Carmel with her husband Frank, is hardworking and ever busy. One of Carolyn's journal entries states, "Laura makes so much possible in my life, doing such a variety of things and such a chirpy personality and disposition. [She is] detailed, organized, loving, [and] sensitive—[a] genius, basically extraordinary."

After John Larson's passing, John Seyler became her Property Manager and, in Carolyn's words, her 'sacred confidante'. He, his wife Sharon, who Carolyn refers to as a 'beloved friend', and one of their sons, Nathan, arrived within a few days of John Larson's passing. Carolyn feels it was 'God-ordained'. Carolyn recounts that John Seyler, on a previous visit, had become most inspired by Carolyn's poetry for her late husband, David Campagna, and had composed various CDs, one with the title, "When the Angels Come." Carolyn says John was an accomplished musician and poet, writing many exceptionally beautiful poems exchanged and inspired by Carolyn.

John Seyler's position has been replaced by Tiger Windwalker. Tiger is a beloved friend, caregiver, and real world manager and fixer of things. At the time he and Carolyn first met, they were both mourning the passing of their mates. They have developed a natural camaraderie together, especially after the winter of 2019 when Carolyn's home and gardens were severely damaged by heavy storms. Under Tiger's supervision, much work and beautification has occurred after this time and paradise has been restored at the property. Additionally, many sacred and enriching communions have been integral to the emergence of Carolyn's most recent paintings. Tiger is also most accomplished with his own published poetry, photography and music. He is a creator of the gorgeous gardens surrounding Carolyn's home and pool. Dale Diesel, who is a skillful artist and worked as a contractor with Tiger for 20 years, now resides on the mountain too.

Carolyn has carried out this creative ritual of writing for her lifetime. Her long creative life is a real endorsement of what Theodore Roethke, American poet and professor, once declared, "When I create, I am true". It is this Tao-lead chosen process and the assistance of her talented and hard-working editors, Patricia Holt and Kirtana, that has spawned almost half a book shelf of her own books, elevated her to the position of Big Sur's prominent living poet and artist, placed her works in a variety of countries and cultures via translators, mainly due to publisher Stanley H. Barkan of Cross-Cultural Communications, who brought her international recognition. Patricia has been essential to the many translations and Kirtana in the editing and organising. I have also been more than happy to connect Carolyn with some of my international contacts.

From 1984 to 2001, she painted about 2000 paintings and hundreds of drawings. Her paintings have been exhibited in museums and used in books and magazines worldwide. In 2001and 2002, publishers for paintings-created calendars, cards, and address books used her artwork, and also distributed her books. There is a continuous exhibiting of her work, juried and otherwise. She has been a pioneer of consciousness culture for most of her adult life.

As well as awards for her poetry, she has won awards for her paintings. Apart from her prodigious output of publications and paintings, she has also produced her *Art Thoughts, Letters to Pops* (poems and prose to her father, with drawings done at the same time), *Revelations* (philosophical poetry and prose,) a collection of fables, as well as other prose and journal collections up to the present. Her poetry constantly appears in international magazines and anthologies; and has won many editorial prizes.

Carolyn has read her poetry in public over the years, often accompanied by a musician, such as British-born Martin Shears and even American poet and artist David Wayne Dunn, once her partner and now a beloved friend of Carolyn's, who has been known to turn up at her live events with a musical instrument. In fact, she and David have done many open mic readings together over the decades, sometimes just showing up spontaneously in a venue, in Monterey or San Francisco, reading their poems, and David accompanying Carolyn with his music. When she came to Wales and London to be the Special Featured Artist at an International Festival at the Dylan Thomas Theatre in Swansea and an event at the Free Word Centre in London, both organized by me, she was accompanied by the late Welsh singer-songwriter Dan Murray.

When she reads, her diction is clear and crisp, her very engaging voice discovering again the rhythms of a lyrical poem's lines, the appropriate pauses, the effective imagery, the message or messages, and the parable of feelings. She has the necessary skills to draw an audience into the personal room of her poetry. She has been known to get caught up in the emotional spaces of her poems and for tears to shine in her eyes, like a singing bird moved by the power of its own sorrow. It can add a touching edge, an unexpected moment of vulnerability to her strong, polished performance.

It is that fragility and strength I saw when watching Carolyn draw at the event in McGowan House. The fragility and strength of someone giving over their being to creating, preoccupied by the tease and call of their imagination.

I first met Carolyn in 2008 when I was on a hectic six weeks tour, the Dylan Thomas Tribute Tour of America, with the late Aeronwy Thomas, poet and writer and the only daughter of Dylan Thomas. The tour was organised by Stanley H. Barkan, a poet and my and Aeronwy's American publisher, in consultation with emeritus professor, poet and critic Vince Clemente. John Dotson was our West Coast host and he organized an event at the Monterey Peninsula College. Carolyn and her partner, poet David Wayne Dunn, attended it. My first writer's residency in her cabin was in the summer of 2010. Since then I have witnessed, particularly via our many conversations, Carolyn's giving herself over to the act of creation and my admiration for her commitment has never wavered. As she has stated, "I am an instrument of creation, not a decider."

So what is Carolyn's journey from a talented young girl to the poet and artist she is today? It is a journey against overwhelming social pressures to fit in to a privileged life, a journey of a young socialite to a reclusive lifestyle, a journey of a woman answering a creative calling from childhood, and a journey of someone who has deservedly and impressively achieved publication, recognition and admiration for her poems and paintings around the world.

Acknowledgements

My special thanks to Carolyn Mary Kleefeld for our stimulating conversations over the years in her Big Sur cabin, where I have resided for two months as a writer-in-residence during the past ten summers, and on our walks on the landscape below her isolated home that, given the solitude and silence, inspired her poetry, prose writings, journal writings, and paintings since she settled there.

Many thanks to Patricia Holt, Kirtana, and Laura Zabrowski who work with Atoms Mirror Atoms, Carolyn's company name, for their invaluable help re: their answers to my questions about facts, writings, paintings, photos, and so many other things. And to Li Yao for designing and the late Michael Zakian, Museum Director at Weisman Museum, Pepperdine University, California for his help with photos.

My thanks to Stanley H. Barkan, poet and Carolyn's and my New York publisher, for his admirable professional diligence whilst checking my whole manuscript of the book for any errors of mine. Also to writer and sculptor John Dotson, who introduced me and Aeronwy Thomas, daughter of Dylan Thomas, to Carolyn at our Monterey Peninsula College event on the West Coast leg of our 2008 Dylan Thomas Tribute Tour of America, organized by Stanley H. Barkan in consultation with emeritus professor and poet Vince Clemente.

Thanks, too, to Carla Kleefeld, Claudia Kleefeld, and Glen Cheda, who is Edmund Kara's trustee.

Last but not least, my thanks to my wife for understanding the far too many hours I spend in my writing room because—as the Irish poet W.B. Yeats said — "Words alone are certain good".

Sources

Carolyn's main published writings are listed below:

Climates of the Mind (poems and philosophical aphorisms). The Horse and Bird Press, Los Angeles, CA, 1979 (4th printing)

Satan Sleeps with the Holy: Word Paintings (poems). The Horse and Bird Press, Los Angeles, CA, 1982

Lovers in Evolution (poems and photographs from Mt. Palomar Observatory). The Horse and Bird Press, Los Angeles, CA, 1983

Songs of Ecstasy (art booklet with poems commemorating Carolyn's solo exhibition and poetry reading at Gallerie Illuminati, Santa Monica, CA). Atoms Mirror Atoms, Carmel, CA, 1990

Songs of Ecstasy, Limited Edition (poems), Atoms Mirror Atoms, Carmel, CA, 1990

Mavericks of the Mind: Conversations for the New Millennium (interviews with Allen Ginsberg, Terence McKenna, Timothy Leary, Laura Archera Huxley, Carolyn Mary Kleefeld, et al.), by David Jay Brown and Rebecca Novick. The Crossing Press, Freedom, CA, 1993; 2nd edition by Maps, Santa Cruz, CA, 2010

The Alchemy of Possibility: Reinventing Your Personal Mythology (prose, poems and art, with quotes from the Tarot and *I Ching*; can serve as an oracle). Foreword by Laura Archera Huxley. Merrill-West Publishing, Carmel, CA, 1998; 2nd edition, 2013 See *alchemyoracle.com*

Kissing Darkness: Love Poems and Art (poems and art), Co-authored with David Wayne Dunn. RiverWood Books, Ashland, OR, 2003

Carolyn Mary Kleefeld: Visions from Big Sur (catalog from exhibit, Frederick R. Weisman Museum of Art). Art with commentary by Michael Zakian, PhD. Pepperdine University, Malibu, CA, 2008

Soul Seeds: Revelations and Drawings (philosophical aphorisms and art). Foreword by Laura Archera Huxley. Cross-Cultural Communications, Merrick, New York, 2008

Vagabond Dawns (poems, with CD). Foreword by David Wayne Dunn, Prologue by Professor-Doctor Bernfried Nugel. Cross-Cultural Communications, Merrick, New York, 2009

Psyche of Mirrors: A Promenade of Portraits (prose, poems, and art). Preface by Peter Thabit Jones, Introduction by Vince Clemente, Foreword by Deanna McKinstry-Edwards. The Seventh Quarry/Cross-Cultural Communications, Wales, UK, and Merrick, New York, 2012

Vagabond Dawns (English/Korean bilingual edition) (poems). Translated by Irene Seonjoo Yoon. Korean Expatriate Literature/Cross-Cultural Communications, Los Angeles, California, and Merrick, New York, 2012

Zori Hoinari - Vagabond Dawns (English/Romanian bilingual edition) (poems). Foreword by Alexandru Zotta, Translated by Dr. Olimpia Iacob. Limes Publishing, Cluj, Romania, 2013

The Divine Kiss: An Exhibit of Paintings and Poems (poems and art). Foreword by Darin Deterra, PhD. Cross-Cultural Communications/The Seventh Quarry Press, Merrick, New York, and Wales, UK, 2014

The Divine Kiss/In the Flames of Dandelions (Sărut Divin/În Flăcările Păpădilor) (English/Romanian bilingual edition) (poems). Co-authored with Ioan Nistor. All poems translated by Dr. Olimpia Iacob. Limes Publishing, Cluj, Romania, 2014

Soul Seeds: Revelations and Drawings (English/Korean bilingual edition) (philosophical aphorisms and art). Translated by Dr. Byoung K. Park. Korean Expatriate Literature/Cross-Cultural Communications, Los Angeles, California, and Merrick, New York , 2014

Soul Seeds: Revelations and Drawings (English/Japanese bilingual edition) (philosophical aphorisms and art). Translated by Naoshi Koriyama. Coal Sack Publishing/Cross-Cultural Communications, Tokyo, Japan, and Merrick, New York, 2014

Soul Seeds: Revelations and Drawings (Sicilian/English/Italian trilingual edition) (philosophical aphorisms and art). Translated by Gaetano Cipolla. Legas Publishing (in cooperation with Cross-Cultural Communications), Mineola, New York, 2014

The Divine Kiss (English/Japanese bilingual edition) (poems and art). Translated by Naoshi Koriyama. Coal Sack Publishing/Cross-Cultural Communications, Tokyo, Japan and Merrick, New York, 2017

The Divine Kiss (English/Sicilian/Italian trilingual edition) (poems and art). Translated by Marco Scalabrino and Gaetano Cipolla. Legas Publishing/Cross-Cultural Communications Mineola, and Merrick, New York, 2018

The Divine Kiss (English/Greek bilingual edition) (poems and art). Translated by Manolis Aligizakis. Libros Libertad Publishing and Cross-Cultural Communications Surrey, BC, Canada and Merrick, New York 2018

The Divine Kiss (English/Persian bilingual edition) (poems and art) Translated by Sepideh Zamani. Published by Mehri Publication Ltd/Cross Cultural Communications London, United Kingdom, Merrick, New York, 2021

Soul Seeds: Revelations and Drawings (English/Spanish bilingual edition) (philosophical aphorisms and art) Translated by Kristine Doll. Saldonar Publishing/Cross-Cultural Communications, Barcelona, Spain and Merrick, New York 2021

Soul Seeds: Revelations and Drawings (English/Catalan bilingual edition) (philosophical aphorisms and art) Translated by August Bover. Saldonar Publishing/Cross-Cultural Communications, Barcelona, Spain and Merrick, New York 2021

Immortal Seeds (Poems and Art). Cross-Cultural Communications/The Seventh Quarry Press, Merrick, New York, and Wales, UK, 2022

I have also had access to many of Carolyn's unpublished writings and access to some of her unpublished journals (2001-2016)

www.carolynmarykleefeld.com
www.alchemyoracle.com

Selected Books

Auden, W. H. *Collected Poems* (London: Faber and Faber, 1991)

Brown, David Jay/McClen Novick, Rebecca (eds.), *Mavericks of the Mind: Conversations for the New Millennium* (Freedom, California: The Crossing Press, 1993)

Brown, David Jay/ Hill, Rebecca Ann (eds.) *Women of Visionary Art* (Vermont: Inner Traditions/Park Street Press, 2018)

Charters, Ann (editor). *The Penguin Book of The Beats* (London: Penguin, 1993)

Heaney, Seamus. *Preoccupations: Selected Prose 1968-1978 (London: Faber and Faber, 1984)*

Karman, James. *Robinson Jeffers/Poet and Prophet* (California: Stanford University Press, 2015)

Miller, Henry. *Big Sur and the Oranges of Hieronymus Bosch* (New York: New Directions, 1957)

Plath, Sylvia. *The Bell Jar* (London: Faber and Faber, 2005)

Skelton, Robin. *The Practice of Poetry* London: Heinemann Educational Books, 1971)

Thabit Jones, Peter. (Ed.) *The Seventh Quarry Swansea Poetry Magazine*/Special Supplement: An Interview with David Campagna by John Dotson (Wales: The Seventh Quarry Press, 2016)

Thomas, Dylan. *Collected Poems* (London: W. enfield & Nicolson, 2003)

Thomas, Edward. *Collected Poems* (London: Faber and Faber, 2004)

Wordsworth, William. *The Collected Poems of William Wordsworth* (London: Wordsworth Editions, 1994)

Yeats, W. B. *The Collected Works in Verse and Prose of William Butler Yeats* (South Carolina: BiblioLife, 2009)

Yeats, W. B. *The Poems Collected Works of W. B. Yeats* (New Jersey: Prentice Hall & IBD, 1997)

www.edmundkara.com
www.visitcalifornia.com

List of illustrations

1. Carolyn Mary Kleefeld (Photo: Not known © Carolyn Mary Kleefeld Collection)

2. Carolyn Mary Kleefeld (Photo: Not known © Carolyn Mary Kleefeld Collection)

3. Catford's famous town-centre cat sculpture (Photo: Love Catford SE6/Borough of Lewisham)

4. Front cover of *The Nanose in Nanoseland* (Photo: Carolyn Mary Kleefeld © Carolyn Mary Kleefeld Collection)

5. Page from *The Nanose in Nanoseland* (Photo: Carolyn Mary Kleefeld © Carolyn Mary Kleefeld Collection)

6. The young ballerina (Photo: Not known © Carolyn Mary Kleefeld Collection)

7. The tennis girl at the Racquet Club, Palm Springs (Photo: Not known © Carolyn Mary Kleefeld Collection)

8. The beautiful young socialite (Photo: Not known © Carolyn Mary Kleefeld Collection)

9. The world traveller (Photo: Not known © Carolyn Mary Kleefeld Collection)

10. The memorial plaques to Amelia Taper at Hillside Memorial Park (Photo: Hillside Memorial Park)

11. Carolyn and Travis Kleefeld, actor and singer (Photo: Not known © Carolyn Mary Kleefeld Collection)

12. Claudia and Carla Kleefeld (Photo: Not known © Carolyn Mary Kleefeld Collection)

13. Carolyn with her daughters, Claudia and Carla (Photo:Not known © Carolyn Mary Kleefeld Collection)

14. Carla Kleefeld (Photo: Carla Kleefeld © Carla Kleefeld)

15. Claudia and her daughter Chiara at Chiara's 16th Gatsby Birthday party (Photo: Claudia Kleefeld © Claudia Kleefeld)

16. Dr. Carl Faber, psychologist, lecturer, and poet of UCLA (Photo: Not known © Not known)

17. Carolyn with the manuscript of *Climates of the Mind* (Photo: Not known © Carolyn Mary Kleefeld Collection)

18. Carolyn with a copy of her first book, *Climates of the Mind* (Photo: Photo: Not known © Carolyn Mary Kleefeld Collection)

19. Big Sur (Photo: Peter Thabit Jones © Peter Thabit Jones)

20. Big Sur (Photo: Peter Thabit Jones © Peter Thabit Jones)

21. Part of the large room of Carolyn's home where she paints and works (Photo: Peter Thabit Jones © Peter Thabit Jones)

List of Plates

Artist Statement - Carolyn Mary Kleefeld

Art, like music, offers a language beyond words. To be innovative, it must be created from an inner wilderness, free of stale and redundant concepts.

If art arises from an inner necessity to express rather than from a preconceived idea of beauty or style, then it can reflect, in symbolic imagery, our primal nature and oneness with all things.

Through the instrument of my being, I let my intuition choose color and form, an experiment comparable to musical improvisation.

For me art is a spontaneous journey on the crest of the Tao's wave, an exploration born of passion, spawned by the Mystery. Initially, I am the maiden falling in love– then later, the ruthless editor-analyst.

Ultimately art is an innocent interactive mirror of my innermost process, whisking me out of time into the Timeless. My life's passion is to create art from this unconditioned well of being and to inspire such a journey in others.

"When I set out to find myself, I created someone, I discovered someone beyond my imagination. So in losing myself, I created myself."
—*Carolyn Mary Kleefeld*

"My art provides an inner-active mirror, revealing in symbolic meaning, archetypal themes, glimpses of my soul."
—*Carolyn Mary Kleefeld*

Carolyn Mary Kleefeld © Carolyn Mary Kleefeld Collection

Chapter 1

CHILDHOOD

"flames of my ancestors glow/through my being"
—*Carolyn Mary Kleefeld*

Carolyn Mary Kleefeld was born in Catford, England. Catford, is a district of South West London, within the London Borough of Lewisham. Nowadays, a giant fiberglass sculpture of a black-and-white cat clings to a black support, which juts out between buildings and is emblazoned with the welcoming words CATFORD CENTRE. It certainly makes the entrance to Catford's shopping centre a distinctive, if unusual and slightly humorous, experience.

The giant cat sculpture in Catford © 2017 Love Catford
SE6/Borough of Lewisham

It is said that the name of Catford possibly originates from the place where cattle, in Saxon times, crossed the River Thames. Another theory is that the name comes from all-black cats being tossed into the ford because of their connection to witchcraft.

Carolyn was actually born on the kitchen table of her parents' home in Catford. The youngest child of Mark and Amelia Taper, who were Jewish immigrants to Britain, Carolyn was one of three children. Her brother Barry being five and a half years older, followed by her sister Janice, who was three and a half years older. Carolyn has retained a lifelong affection for England, her birthplace. She did, in fact, return to Catford as an adult in June 2013, with her then partner and eventual husband, David Campagna. Catford, though, by then had changed from what she remembered as a small child.

Three years before Carolyn was born, the Broadway Theatre had opened. An art deco building, it is now a Grade II listed structure because of its architectural and historic interest. Among notable people connected with Catford, is Ernest Dowson (1867–1900), an English poet, novelist, and short story writer, who lived and died in the district. A member of the 'Rhymers Club', which was founded by the great Irish poet W. B. Yeats and Ernest Rhys, a writer with Welsh ancestry, he was connected with the Decadent movement, an aesthetic ideology of excess and artificiality in the late 19th century in Western Europe which later spread to the United States. American author Margaret Mitchell used a phrase from a Dowson poem for her famous novel, *Gone with the Wind*.

Catford, one imagines, would have been a dramatic change of environment for Carolyn's parents when one considers their origins. Carolyn's father S. (Sydney) Mark Taper was born on 25th December in 1901 and died on 16th December 1994. Born in Poland, where one grandfather was a rabbi, his family left Poland for England when he was a year old to escape persecution. He grew up in a Jewish ghetto, his family poor, and the language all around him was 'old world' Yiddish. As a schoolboy, Mark was put in charge of teaching younger boys after their teachers left to become soldiers in the First World War. He quit school at twelve years of age and began helping his father to make officer soldiers' uniforms. At sixteen, he replaced his father as manager at the plant, after his father was injured in a German bombing raid on London. Mark's only escape was to make so much money that his anxious reactions to the landlord demanding the rent every month would never happen to him and his future family again.

A conservative and self-governed gentleman, he used his extraordinary innate genius and industrious approach to establish a successful chain of shoe stores in London after acquiring a shoe shop in 1920. By1926, at the age of 25, he was financially secure and able to retire. However, he went back into education to learn surveying and appraising. In 1929, he bought a real estate business from two partners who were retiring.

He began investing very successfully in real estate and house building and the wealth he accrued gave him a substantial financial portfolio. One development in Brockley, South London, was named after his wife Amelia's nickname (Milly), Millward Road, which is now Milward Grove; and another was named after his son, Barrydale, now Barriedale. Unlike other British real estate agents, he sent his agents around in cars to show potential buyers properties, thus giving a personal and better service to such buyers. By the 1930s he had achieved success as a property builder.

In a position to retire again, he decided that he and his wife and three children should move to America. He had lived in London for thirty-six years. He later told *The Times* newspaper, "I thought I ought to spend more time with my family. And I was looking for the secret paradise we all seek, free from pressure and care".

It is clear, too, that Adolf Hitler's organised and evil anti-Semitism and the widespread fears of a quickly changing Germany, a Germany becoming so hostile to Jewish people, played a major part in his decision to leave Britain with his family. In fact within a month or so after their move, a bomb struck their house in London as Britain suffered the German bombing offensive from 7th September 1940 to 10th May1941, known as the Blitz, during the Second World War.

Carolyn recalls that her English Nanny, Dorothy Rolfe, nicknamed 'Dodo' and who was her Nanny until she was 11 years old, told her one day that they were going on holiday. It was, of course, a permanent move, but no one explained anything to Carolyn. They sailed on the RMS Queen Mary, which was the flagship transatlantic ocean liner of the Cunard Line from May 1936 to October 1946. During the long journey, then around four days, her mother arranged a surprise birthday party for Carolyn. When Carolyn, aged 4, arrived, she said, "I don't know a soul here" and left. When she returned to her bunk, she thought, 'Now I won't get any gifts'. Later in life, Carolyn reflected, "I had been separated from my native England and brought to America—a major upheaval at an early age". Carolyn has said that even then she had a mind of her own and always followed her inner promptings.

They spent the first few months in New York and Carolyn's mother would stick to her traditional English tea afternoons in the new country. The family then took a cross-country train ride that ended at Union Station in Downtown Los Angeles. On the way to Santa Monica, Mark told the cab driver to take them to a beach. The cab driver told Mark and Amelia that the best place to find sand and sun was Long Beach and drove them there. The Tapers lived in the penthouse of Long Beach's Huntington Hotel (for $80 a month at the time) and the children enjoyed playing on the sand in the constant sunshine, a dramatic change from the often rain-washed, grey and chilly world of Britain. Around this time, the remarkably benevolent Tapers were also bringing hundreds of Jewish and Catholic refugee children out of Nazi Germany to settle in Britain and the United States, saving them from the persecution by Hitler's determined and clinical program. It was an incredibly humane gesture by Mark and Amelia at a time of such institutionalized and inhumane evil.

Mark Taper was not the type of man who could settle into retirement or spend more time with his family. He said in 1965, "I suppose that is the story of my life. Whenever I thought of retiring, some new need appeared, some job had to be done". Two landowners, who were retiring, offered him 20-acre slices of Long Beach for $6,000 and $5,700. He skillfully arranged 400 lots and, unable to find a builder, decided to build the homes himself. There was a post-war housing boom in Southern California and Mark Taper became the founder of Biltmore Homes, which began building affordable houses for World War Two soldiers returning home to Long Beach, Norwalk, Compton, and Lakewood. The houses were for low and middle-income people and he built 35,000 properties, which was one of the largest of such housing developments in the United States. His astonishing financial genius also assisted him in founding the First Charter Financial Corporation of Beverly Hills. The Corporation had become the nation's second biggest publicly held savings and loan holding company by the late 1960s. His impeccable timing made him able to be the last to start a Savings and Loan.

Long Beach, a coastal city in Southern California and one of the world's largest shipping ports, was the Taper's first home in America. The RMS Queen Mary, the very ocean liner that Mark Taper and his family boarded to make their new life in America, is now permanently docked at Long Beach. It was bought by the City of Long Beach in 1967 and is now used as a hotel and maritime museum. It is interesting that Carolyn's father knew where to go in America and where to start the house-building empire he would create. He, his wife, and their children would eventually be granted American citizenship. Carolyn says that at the time she did not like the fact that she wasn't asked if she wanted to go and live in America: although now her archive and museum are there.

PLATE 1

1. Mark and Amelia Taper © Carolyn Mary Kleefeld Collection

2. Toddler Carolyn © Carolyn Mary Kleefeld Collection

3. Barry, Janice, and Carolyn © Carolyn Mary Kleefeld Collection

4. The beauty contest winner © Carolyn Mary Kleefeld Collection

5. The Taper family © Carolyn Mary Kleefeld Collection

6. The family home © Carolyn Mary Kleefeld Collection

A desire to have a home close to the beach, meant a move for the Taper family again, within a mere six months of their arrival into this country, to a new property in Santa Monica, a coastal city west of downtown Los Angeles. Located on Santa Monica Bay, it boasts a Mediterranean climate that can see its inhabitants experience around 310 days of sunshine each year. The Santa Monica Pier, a 1600-foot-long concrete structure, opened to the public in 1909 and has remained a popular tourist attraction and the pride of residents. It has featured in films such as *The Sting* (1973) and *Titanic* (1997).

Carolyn would later comment on their move to America in a 2012 journal entry, after her own visit to London as an adult with her partner and future husband David Campagna, which is full of praise for her father's foresight and bravery in making the decision for his family: "I applaud more than ever what my father was able to do, how he escaped from England, saved our lives from being bombed, moved us to a new frontier, meaning California. How did he know how to do it? [He was] truly a genius and he had great intuitive power and timing in all the things he did—missing the bombing, building vet housing just at the perfect time and going into the Savings and Loan years later when he did, before they stopped allowing it. I can only be deeply grateful now that he brought us from an old battle worn land without space for the future to California, the most progressive state. And that we are living here in a new paradise, a first frontier. How incredibly fortunate we are. I hadn't realized all this before this latest visit over the great 'pond.' Travel can certainly open one's eyes and perspectives. I thank David, who insisted I visit my birthplace".

Carolyn's mother Amelia, whose family surname was Lewis, which was probably an Anglicised form of the Jewish name Levi or Levy, and whose father was a musician in Portugal, was a talented artist who worked for London's *Vogue* on a freelance basis. The first British issue of the sister publication of America's *Vogue* appeared in 1916. Dorothy Todd, who became its second editor, introduced a mix of fashion and the arts, and there were contributions from the likes of Virginia Woolf and Aldous Huxley, whose wife Laura would eventually become a beloved friend of Carolyn's. Pen-and-ink illustrations, which Amelia would have contributed, dominated the fashion magazines until post-World War Two, before taking second place to the overwhelming and appealing technological advances of photography. Amelia once told Carolyn with regard to her abandoning her artwork, "I gave it up to have children." Something that Carolyn at the time vowed never to do herself.

Carolyn inherited her mother's artistic talents and creative sensitivities, whilst Barry and Janice, her siblings, grew up to follow their father's mindset via business careers. In the familial furnace of a businessman father and a creative mother, lifelong dualities, complex and challenging, would forge Carolyn Mary Kleefeld, international artist and poet.

Highly imaginative at a young age, Carolyn found solace in habitual reading and drawing. She has stated, "I arrived in this world with a rich imagination and the need to express it. From there, the muse bemused me, making surprise visits."[1]

Precocious and energetic, she also displayed her acting skills when she entertained her mother's friends with her live performances of impersonations of her own made-up characters. At just nine years-old, Carolyn wrote and illustrated her first book, *The Nanose in Nanoseland*. The inspiration for it was her watching dust particles dancing in a sunbeam flooding her bedroom window. In an early sign of her highly individual and original way of looking at things, she turned each speck of dust into a micro person and even thought of the world where they lived. As a child, the drawings of them filled the walls of her pink bedroom.

The front cover of The Nanose in Nanoseland
© Carolyn Mary Kleefeld Collection

A page from The Nanose in Nanoseland
© Carolyn Mary Kleefeld Collection

Later in life, Carolyn would realize she was touching on nanotechnology in that childhood creation of Nanoseland: "Through my impression of the dancing particles, I had my first recorded interaction with atomic life. My art was the bridge translating localized conception (dust particles) into atomic theory. I thus experienced intimate dialogue with the quantum universe. I find it fascinating that my poetic imagination discovered this word as a nine-year-old before I had any knowledge of its meaning. To me, this confirms the existence of a gnostic reservoir of wisdom that can be tapped into whenever we are inquiring and receptive. Actually, the word *education*, from the Latin root *educare*, means 'to bring out that which is within'".

The personal and the universal would become a major theme in the art and writings produced by Carolyn.

Carolyn attended the Franklyn Elementary School, named after Benjamin Franklin, one of the Founding Fathers of the United States. She did experience some anti-Semitism at this time in her neighborhood and was even called the derogatory word 'kike'. Her education there was followed by time spent at Westlake School for Girls. Established in 1904 by Jessica Smith Vance and Frederica de Laguna, the exclusive school originally catered for females only and served elementary and secondary education. In 1991, Westlake School for Girls merged with Harvard School for Boys, creating Harvard-Westlake School, now located in west Los Angeles. Past famous pupils of Westlake School for Girls includes legendary child film star Shirley Temple (1928–2014) and film star Elizabeth Montgomery (1933–1995), who is renowned for starring in *Bewitched*, the popular American sitcom.

Young Carolyn needed physical as well as imaginative expression. She became a prima ballerina, and riding Mabel, her beloved horse, whom she has described as her 'primary love', were two ways of achieving such tangible enjoyment and freedom. Carolyn and Mabel would go on to winning many horse shows and many trophies. She had such unusual energy and she applied her Olympic-type energy into many sports. Carolyn's parents bought Mabel from Snowy Baker, an Australian-born actor and Olympic medal-winning boxer, who lived at The Riviera Country Club. An all-round sportsman, Snowy was excellent at horsemanship and taught the likes of Rudolph Valentino, Douglas Fairbanks, Greta Garbo, Shirley Temple, and Elizabeth Taylor to ride. Carolyn met him at The Riviera Country Club. Mabel cost $75.00, about $1,000 dollars now.

It was listening to the music of Tchaikovsky that inspired Carolyn's love of dancing. From the age of five to the age of twelve, Carolyn attended the Toland School of Ballet in Santa Monica, a short walk from Downtown Santa Monica and just minutes from the ocean. Here she was the prima ballerina.

The young ballerina © Carolyn Mary Kleefeld Collection

Carolyn has said she learned to dance by observing other dancers, rather than by what she was told to do in the classes. She reached a level in dance where an invitation to study at The Bolshoi Ballet School came about. Established as an orphanage by order of Catherine II in 1763, Bolshoi is the oldest theatrical school in Moscow. The first dance classes took place in 1773. Her mother Amelia, though, disapproved of such overseas travel for someone so young. Amelia's decision could have also been powered by her knowledge of a Europe darkened by the Second World War, and the Holocaust and the unfolding Cold War between America and the Soviet Union. Carolyn was very discomforted, at the time and even into adulthood, by her mother's decision. It was only recently that she saw the whole thing from her mother's perspective. Also, Amelia had two other children at home and could not have accompanied Carolyn.

Like most potential writers, Carolyn was an avid reader of books as a young girl. When she was around twelve years old, she came across the writings of Guy de Maupassant, the 19th-century French short story writer. Henry-René Guy de Maupassant (1850–1893) is regarded as the greatest French short story writer. Gustave Flaubert (1821–1880), the great French novelist and 'father' of the realist school of French literature, became a mentor to the young Henry-René. Maupassant, one of the naturalist school of writers, also wrote poetry and novels and influenced writers such as Russia's Anton Chekhov and America's Henry James. Carolyn has said that Maupassant was her first love in literature.

She also read fantasy fiction and the works of Wolo, a pseudonym for Baron Wolf Ehrardt Anton George Trutzshuler von Falkenstein. Born of nobility in Berlin in 1902, he moved to the USA in 1922 and became an exchange student at the University of Wisconsin. He settled in Los Angeles in 1927, where he set up his art studio. Self-taught, he went on to San Francisco and worked on the *San Francisco Chronicle* as a caricaturist-columnist for many years. He died in San Francisco in 1989.

Published in the 1940s, Wolo's books for children are *Amanda*, *Sir Archibald*, *Tweedles Be Brave*, *Friendship Valley*, and *The Secret of the Ancient Oak*. His five books, illustrated by him, utilized mythic figures and imaginary realms, and he filled Carolyn's world with the extraordinary. She would do the latter for readers of her future poetry and viewers of her future art.

Her later artistic explorations of fantasy were her vivid imagination needing an outer "reality" to match her inner reality. She would write in her book *The Alchemy of Possibility*, published in 1998, "I see that in my childhood I was engaged in the same primary activities as now. How my mind and imagination worked is recorded in my early letters, drawings, and stories revealing the nucleus, the psychology of whom I am now. I see that I always had a passion for wilderness and wildlife, that I was a born wanderer intuitively drawn to discovery through observing the natural world, people and myself. A great curiosity always propelled my mind."

As a young girl, Carolyn showed a unique compassion towards living things. Her older brother Barry would kill ants to get her attention and make her scream. Feeling sorry for them, Carolyn would place each one on cotton wool, bury it in a matchbox, then put a cross on its grave and she would sing to their graves. She considers the small tombs to be among her earliest forms of creative expression. As a child she was also intrigued with the butterfly cocoons attached to an outer wall of the home where she grew up in Santa Monica. Her observations of caterpillars evolving into butterflies had a profound effect on her, serving as a metaphoric omen of what eventually would become her life-long fascination with transformation.

Christmas was a special time then and as Carolyn has written in her journals, "For me, as a child, I loved having my pillow cases filled with things. I usually had oranges, nuts and not gift things in it, but it was just as pleasant when filled up with such treats. And I remembered waiting up all night for Santa Claus one night. I was innocent and naïve and it was fun then. But then I was disappointed (no Santa)".

Formal education's conveyor-belt of churning out small boys and small girls who will fit into society has never catered to those children who are different, and Carolyn was one of those who could not naturally and easily progress along the rigid system, despite her obvious intelligence and desire to learn about things. This uneasiness was in her throughout all her years of education. As she would eventually admit in *The Alchemy of Possibility*, "I have always been fatigued by public systems, schools, and universities. I daydreamed my way through school, but was always fascinated by art and psychology. I found the subtler sensitivities of the natural world and its creatures more entrancing than academia."

It was also around this time, when Carolyn was about eleven years old, that her English Nanny, Dorothy Rolfe, nicknamed 'Dodo', who was like a mother to Carolyn, left her employment with the Taper family, which was an obvious emotional blow to a young girl trying to find her feet in a new country and a different way of living. Carolyn has said that she had little closeness with her family. Her older brother teased both sisters sadistically.

Having extremely high energy, "ready to be in the Olympics" Carolyn recalls, which she has described as possible high anxiety, Carolyn found it insufferable to be, in her own words, imprisoned in school everyday. For the schoolgirl Carolyn, freedom was waiting outside, beyond the classroom windows and door; and freedom for her was her soul mate, her beloved horse Mabel, with whom she has said she took on a magical alliance.

Developers were yet to alter raw areas of Los Angeles for habitation, so Carolyn could ride Mabel into the local canyons, such as Mandeville Canyon, a small community situated in the Brentwood neighborhood of Los Angeles, which became well known as a horse riding and hiking landscape. During the early 1940s, the canyon became a rural neighborhood for notable and wealthy people, who were keen on horse and playing polo at Will Rogers State Park, the former home of American humorist Will Rogers, which became a State Park in 1944.

On her horse-riding adventures with Mabel, Carolyn would sometimes meet the young Jane Fonda, the future actress, who would be out and about riding her horse. Jane was blowing Double Bubble gum, which to Carolyn was the treat beyond a treat. Carolyn and Mabel would also venture from the Riviera Country Club to Brentwood Country Club where Carolyn took tennis lessons. In fact, she kept score for the polo players at the Riviera Country Club. She would climb up some stairs into a wooden room and handle the chukker's score. She enjoyed doing this task and she loved the view of the polo ponies and open fields they played upon.

The Riviera Country Club, which is situated in Pacific Palisades, is renowned as an exclusive private club and its championship golf course. The child star Elizabeth Taylor trained for her role in the 1944 film *National Velvet* at the Riviera Equestrian Center. Past famous club members include Humphrey Bogart, Walt Disney, and Gregory Peck. The Hillcrest Country Club, among others such as the Brentwood Country Club, came about because Jewish people were not allowed to become members of the Los Angeles Country Club and The Wilshire Country Club, so they established their own clubs.

Carolyn rode Mabel in riding competitions, winning many trophies and ribbons at such places as the Riviera Country Club. During her and Mabel's riding escapades, Carolyn would sometimes climb into the rafters of the tack rooms, which are rooms in or near a stable that are used for storing saddles, harnesses etc., and she would fill up a gunny sack, with treats that jockeys had from the stables and she would feed Mabel with them. She also trained her horse Mabel to jump and would ride her bareback and without a bridle. All she needed from Carolyn for direction was Carolyn's hand on her mane awhile with a little pressure. Cars would line up on Sunset Boulevard to watch young Carolyn jumping Mabel without a saddle or bridle.

At this time Carolyn was writing about Mabel all the time, until a family friend told her she should write every day but be disciplined. This bit of advice stopped Carolyn in her tracks and she did not write anything for a while. Discipline meant rules and Carolyn, even then, loved the freedom of a necessity to write, letting her thoughts and ideas flow like a free and rhythmic river.

She would take her red wagon down to the stables and sold drinks to the field workers. She gave neighborhood children rides in her red wagon and told them stories she made up about rides through the Amazon jungle. She even sold the children old comic books at a bargain price along with charging for the fantasy rides.

She recalls that she never had any money to buy the delicious-looking hot nuts at the corner pharmacy on Santa Monica Boulevard, although she did make her own pocket money weeding the neighbor's gardens. One time Carolyn spent hours tying some kind of vine up on little sticks. Then the neighbor came out and said she was trying to tie a vine up that wasn't meant to be like that, so Carolyn was not paid. She didn't repeat any work like that again.

Carolyn was always seeking adventure in any shape or form, especially if it were a physical challenge. As she recalls in a journal entry, ". . . my childhood at the pier and on the Merry Go Round, and the Jonathan club with my first high-flying dive, and being embarrassed about my first signs of puberty with a little hair under my arms when I raised my arms for the big dive. The pool looked so far away, I remember, and now I realize it took bravery to make that plunge so far away."

It was, though, also at this time that Carolyn connected deeply with nature and with animals. Her young outdoor adventures, to quote William Wordsworth's *Lines composed a few miles above Tintern Abbey,* allowed her to see "something far more deeply interfused" in her surroundings and, to quote the Wordsworth poem again, she became "A lover of the meadows and the woods /And mountains; and all that we behold / From this green earth".[2]

The Wordsworth association is very relevant as Emeritus Professor Vince Clemente would eventually intimate in his Introduction to Carolyn's book *Psyche of Mirrors: A Promenade of Portraits,* that she was the Wordsworth of Big Sur.[3]

This childhood connection to nature, the awareness of "something far more deeply interfused", is an epiphanic experience that can be attributed to many poets when they were young children. The sense of "bright shoots of everlastingness", a phrase from Henry Vaughan's poem *The Retreat,* in the living landscape can have a profound impact on the heart and soul of a sensitive child. The feeling of "the other", of nature being an affirmation of eternity, is something they will cling to throughout their life's journey. Once experienced by the child, there is an unquiet stirring forever in their being. It is as if a curtain that is veiling so-called reality has been pulled open and a sense of the divine pours into the child's heart. It is a humbling experience.

Young Carolyn found a belief in natural forms and its life forces. The rudder of many of her adult writings and artwork to come would be a realization that the personal is fused to the universal and that the universal is fused to the personal; and that nature is the furniture of holiness, the picturesque and the 'red in tooth and claw', to quote poet Alfred Lord Tennyson. She would develop a Wordsworthian awareness to being the solitary observer. She would become a pantheist. As Carl Faber, the renowned American psychologist, would write in his Foreword to Carolyn's *Satan Sleeps with the Holy* book, "Welling up in her work is the poetess moved and carried by Nature in all its forms."

Chapter 2

TEENAGE YEARS

✧

"I always found my own life."
—Carolyn Mary Kleefeld

Carolyn was fifteen years old when the family moved to the exclusive Beverly Hills, another rung up the social ladder as her father's businesses expanded. A city in California's Los Angeles County, Beverly Hills is synonymous with wealth and Hollywood stars. But, in the early 1900s, non-whites were prohibited from owning or renting property, and Jews were prohibited from selling or renting property.

It is a place of opulence, stretch limos, magnificent multi-million dollar mansions, deluxe shopping areas like Rodeo Drive and very posh restaurants and hotels, such as Planet Hollywood and the famous The Beverly Hills Hotel, known as 'The Pink Palace'. It is home to the Academy of Motion Picture Arts & Sciences and the Museum of Television and Radio.

Not impressed by the neighborhood's visual endorsement of wealth, and the new luxury of her parents' home, Carolyn felt conflicted with her growing sense of her spiritual needs. She felt undermined by the Beverly Hills materialistic values. Many writers in their youth feel unable to fit into the community of their teenage years. They often question the hypocrisy and the perceived falseness of the reality that surrounds them. One thinks of Dylan Thomas and his poem 'I have longed to move away', referring to a desire to leave (for him) the provincial smugness of middle-class Swansea. Such conflict in Carolyn would become the seeds that would grow into a lifetime's need to explore the fathomless tides of her heart.

An outdoor kind of a girl who felt like a tomboy, she found that the materialistic world she found herself in collided with her even then pantheistic approach to the world, her deep love of nature and animals. She would recall in Chapter 41 of her book *The Alchemy of Possibility*, ". . . in Beverly Hills from the age of fifteen, I saw and experienced the shallow void of the superficial. Those who acquire financial excess are often tyrannized by their possessions, burdened by the endless maintenance and accompanying anxieties. I grew up in a world that put material values before the individual, before feeling. One's appearance, one's car, one's home were most important."

She also felt like someone without any real roots. She has stated, "There was no dialogue in my family about our country—the one we left [or the] new one, no dialogue at all really about anything. It was like growing up in a remote land that had no name and that was all my creation, at least emotionally. Although there were all the lovely trees and stables I'd run to, they were a backdrop for my own huge energy and feelings. They never really communicated. I remember the vacant lot across the street, how I loved to walk barefoot and barelegged up to my knees in the mud when it rained. That vacant lot was quite a metaphor for my life at that time, as I really created out of a vacancy, meaning no family communication, no teaching, no roots."

That 'huge energy' would see her jump over all the high hedges on her way to school.

Carolyn took to playing tennis with the same enthusiasm she had taken to horseback-riding and was as successful as she had been as a competitive horseback-rider. She was number one in Beverly Hills as a tournament tennis player and in Santa Monica, and she was referred to as the "dark horse" when she seemed to appear from nowhere to win the "15 and Under" and "18 and Under" women's titles. She was kicked off the Beverly Hills High tennis team when, after she won first place, the teacher asked her to play in third place against another school and she refused to do that. She felt she had earned the right to play number one since she had won the first place position. This defiant spirit and questioning of authority was there throughout Carolyn's life.

Even when she eventually moved to Malibu, she would continue playing tennis. She has said, "One of the lifetimes ago, at a highly creative cycle while residing in Malibu, I entered the annual tennis tournament there. This doubles competition had been won for 20 years by a tall, self-assuming blonde woman whose brother knew how to call every shot in her favor. My partner turned out to be a neighbor from my childhood days in Santa Monica. He was a good tennis player and had a flair for life. We won rather seamlessly and enjoyed drinking a cold beer as we sauntered through. The champ of the past could only utter, "Oh, we over-trained," as she glumly walked away. And my friend and I chuckled to ourselves and drank another beer."

The tennis girl at the Racquet Club, Palm Springs
© Carolyn Mary Kleefeld Collection

It was after the move to Beverly Hills that Carolyn had her beloved old and ailing horse Mabel put to sleep. She had had to leave Mabel in Santa Monica and visit her on bus trips, which Carolyn found frustrating and inconvenient. Carolyn, in some ways, disconnected from that wild and unconventional part of herself, if only temporarily, until she spent time in Malibu and particularly when she moved to Big Sur.

As a teenager, Carolyn liked to listen to Hoagy Carmichael, the American composer, pianist, singer, and bandleader, famous for songs such as *Stardust* and *Georgia on My Mind*. His songs were recorded by many of the iconic singers, such as Frank Sinatra, Nat King Cole, and Ella Fitzgerald. She also liked The Inkspots, an African-American pop vocal group, popular with both black and white audiences.

Another enjoyment at the time was listening to Hunter Hancock (1916–2004), an American disc jockey who was famous for being the first to play rhythm and blues records on the radio and one of the first to broadcast rock 'n' roll records. He was particularly popular with black listeners in Southern California and he made an appearance in the 1957 British film *Rock Around the Clock*.

As an inspired dancer from her early years and with a real passion for music, Carolyn and her boyfriends loved going to see the great entertainers at the swanky night clubs—people such as Billy Daniels, who was notable for the legendary song *That Old Black Magic*, Lena Horne, Nat King Cole, Ella Fitzgerald, and others. During those years she won a dance contest at the Beverly Hills Tennis Club. Her favourite actresses and actors at the time included Marlon Brando, Rita Hayworth, Ava Gardner, James Dean, and Gregory Peck.

Her teen years were challenging. Feeling lost and without guidance, she sought relief with beer drinking, wild parties and boyfriends. Her mother told her she would have less suffering when she was older because of her suffering as a youth. Always popular with boys, Carolyn often had three dates on a weekend night. At one gathering of boys and girls, one boy proposed to her from a phone downstairs while she was upstairs, which she thought was funny. Her girlfriend and she would sit on Carolyn's garden wall at night by the alley and jump into a different boyfriend's car every few hours.

In fact, her group of high school friends was made up of odd girls that didn't fit into the main group. These groups of local boys and girls partied up in the Hollywood Hills, drinking beer, playing music, and dancing bare-footed for hours on the mountain dirt in their rebellious get-togethers. Around this time, Carolyn and her friends, wearing shorts, even gatecrashed a party at the home of the late legendary Hollywood actor Kirk Douglas, who recently died at the age of 103. She recalls that it was great fun. She also became the owner of her first car at this time.

Along with the fun of being a teenager, she was also writing in her journals. Those early journals, though, would later be burned in years to come by a boyfriend. He managed to convince Carolyn she should get rid of her past! She was also reading books on psychology, such as works by Swiss psychiatrist and psychoanalyst Carl G. Jung and German psychologist psychoanalyst Erich Fromm. Barry, her older brother, went into the army, and Janice, her older sister, married at the age of eighteen.

Meanwhile, her formal education continued. In 1950, she attended Beverly Hills High School, where her interest in psychology began, and she graduated from there in 1954. Celebrity alumni includes actors Ronnie Burns, Joel Grey, Carrie Fisher, and singer Lenny Kravitz.

Finding Beverly Hills High boring and without inspiration, she not only didn't enjoy it, she barely got through it. She felt like a "world stranger" (as American journalist, essayist, critic and poet Benjamin De Casseres called himself) in Beverly Hills. Even then, many of the young girls were having plastic surgery on their noses and talking about cashmere sweaters and cars. She felt set aside from such materialistic obsessions. After high school, she attended Santa Monica City College for three years, a public community college, where she began to really learn about Art. Actors James Dean and Dustin Hoffman were former students.

At this time, Carolyn was also travelling with her parents, taking holidays in Florida, Trinidad, Italy, and England. Interestingly, all that Carolyn can recall of their family trip to the Caribbean were the starving dogs at a wharf somewhere and being worried about them—an early example of her compassionate concern for injured or suffering creatures and her love of animals.

Chapter 3

YOUNG ADULTHOOD

"Transcend your own nature like a carp leaping out of the water."
—*Carolyn Mary Keefeld*

Her father's wealth, power and influence meant Carolyn, young and beautiful and available for an expected marriage—was caught up in the web of high society and its accompanying materialism and money. Conforming to the rules of their successful and elitist parents and the wider community, was the mindset of most young women. Carolyn, for a while, played the game of her peer group and via The Beverly Hills Tennis Club in the 1960s, got to know and party with the likes of film producers Richard Zanuck and Joe Pasternak, actors Charlton Heston, Gilbert Roland, Rock Hudson, Paul Newman, Gene Simmons, member of the American rock band Kiss, and singer and actress Dinah Shore. Founded in 1929, the Beverly Hills Tennis Club is famous for its tennis excellence and also offers a swimming pool, sauna, spa, gym, and a restaurant. It attracts some of Hollywood's big names to its courts.   She played tennis with American actor, Gilbert Roland, Pancho Segura, Dinah Shore, and Barbara Sinatra, American model and the fourth wife of Frank Sinatra, and played tennis every day with one of the wives of Tony Curtis.

Years earlier in Santa Monica, Carolyn's tennis teacher had been Ethel Bruce, one of the famous Sutton sisters who dominated the Southern California tennis championships, indeed women's tennis in America in the earliest part of the twentieth century. Ethel, the oldest, won the Southern California's women's championship four times (1906/1911/1912/1913) and published a book, *Tennis Fundamentals and Timing*, co-authored with her husband, Bert O. Bruce, in 1938. The Sutton sisters were so good that someone once made the comment, "It takes a Sutton to beat a Sutton". Carolyn would run to and from her tennis lessons. Once, when Carolyn was waiting for Ethel to give her a lesson, Carolyn was talking to herself and Ethel came upon her and said, "Oh well, as long as you do not answer yourself!"

Carolyn had the necessary attributes, a film star beauty and an engaging and lively personality to be among the Hollywood elite. She even took up paid modeling work as a fashion model and she was on the books of Caroline Leonetti Ltd., a modeling agency. Caroline Leonetti Ahmanson (1918–2005) founded her agency in 1945 in Los Angeles. A fashion consultant on radio and television at the beginning of her career, she was appointed by President Reagan to serve on the President's Committee on the Arts and Humanities.

The beautiful young socialite © Carolyn Mary Kleefeld Collection

The Hollywood actor and film director Cornel Wilde, who starred in such films as *The Greatest Show on Earth,* told Carolyn she had the best body in Beverly Hills and she was asked to do a centerfold for *Playboy* Magazine, which she turned down. A bit later, though, she played in and won a tennis tournament at the Playboy Mansion, *Playboy* magazine founder Hugh Hefner's famous home in Holmby Hills, Los Angeles.

The child who performed impromptu for her mother's friends also had the skills to act. As a young woman Carolyn had an agent at the William Morris Agency, the agency which represented the careers of some of the most iconic figures in entertainment, Charlie Chaplin, Mae West, Al Jolson, Judy Garland, Katharine Hepburn, Elvis Presley, The Beach Boys, The Rolling Stones, and Cher. Carolyn was offered a contract after reading for some of the major Hollywood studios and also did some acting improvisations at The Horseshoe Theater. She admits, though, that she was not very good at memorizing lines and was not really cut out to be an actress. At one point, Carolyn was even named "Queen of the Watermelons" and appeared on *The Art Linkletter Show*, which was hosted by the Canadian-born American radio and television personality. Carolyn recalls one of his sons visiting her after her appearance. She attended movie–mogul parties at the homes of the Zanucks, Richard Darryl, known for films such as *Jaws*, Darryl Francis, known for films such as *How Green Was My Valley*, Joseph Mankowitz, known for such films as *Cleopatra*, and Joe Pasternak, known for films such as *Destry Rides Again*, which starred Marlene Dietrich and James Stewart. She met American author Ray Bradbury one evening at a philanthropic event. She was a friend of Ram Dass, the American spiritual teacher, psychologist and author. He told Carolyn he felt they had known each other forever when they first met.

Carolyn also hung out with actress Hedy Lamarr's boyfriend in Acapulco, Teddy Stauffer, who managed the famous El Miramar hotel. Carolyn and he attended an event where a diver climbed many steps high on a cliff, involving bonfires and festivities before he then dove into the water below. Apparently, Hedy Lamarr appeared the day after one of these events. Carolyn went to Cannes, the resort on the French Riviera, with her mother, where people thought Carolyn was a movie star at the International Film Festival. However, Carolyn recalls she was basically bored with so much of her time there.

She also did water skiing movies, doing ballet on skis for a hotel in Acapulco and in Florida, and hair and fashion assignments on television. As she has stated, she was offered pretty much anything a girl could want, in the Hollywood sense, by the age of twenty-two, acknowledged for her beauty and sexiness, but she felt no connection with her deeper self, which was of no interest to her male pursuers or anyone else.

The world traveller © Carolyn Mary Kleefeld Collection

There is no doubt that she could have gone down the road of glitz and glamour had she really desired to do so. However, like Esther Greenwood in Sylvia Plath's *The Bell Jar*, a fictional character who is really Plath, Carolyn was inwardly battling with the social expectations placed on post-Second World War middle-class and upper-class young women and the creative and spiritual soul she had "put to sleep".

At home, though, from the age of 15 to 22 Carolyn took on the responsibility of being a young caregiver. She took care of her mother who was depressed and alcoholic. School was also painful because Carolyn was always tired because she stayed up late every night to try to help her mother, often finding her passed out on the floor. One night she found her mother bleeding from the nose and fallen flat on the floor. Carolyn called her father but he couldn't respond appropriately and continued to open his mail. He was always too busy building his empire to be a family man or a husband.

So as a young woman, Carolyn's main endeavor was trying to save her mother's life. Her mother died on 23rd May 1958, just two days after her 49th birthday, and two months after Carolyn had married Leonard Harmon, her first husband, whom she met through a friend.

Amelia was buried at a mausoleum at Hillside Memorial Park, Culver City, CA.

The memorial plaques to Amelia Taper at Hillside Memorial Park
© 2018 Hillside Memorial Park

Carolyn says her mother died from a mixture of a cold, alcohol, and sleeping pills. Her mother's death was a horrible shock for Carolyn and she is sure it broke her heart. She studied progressive psychology and spiritual expansion to help heal the trauma. In 2014, when her partner, David Campagna, and later husband and who was battling for his life, Carolyn wrote of her mother:

A Love That Is Stronger Than Death
(for my mother, Amelia)

"As I gaze out over iridescent plains of sea, I feel you in the infinite horizons. Although you departed almost sixty years ago, you are still within me, in my eternal love for you. You sacrificed your life and gifted me with your inheritance, your talents and artist's spirit, your love of flowers, of beauty, your otherworldliness, your humanitarianism.

O my beautiful mother whom I tried to save, you are being saved now through my own depth of healing; for I have discovered a kind of salvation in the sublime blessing of eternal love bestown—a love which is stronger than death, and which now is yours to embrace."

Carolyn and Leonard divorced in 1959. She felt threatened when her husband became mentally unstable and got into financial problems with her father. So, in her mid-twenties, Carolyn felt lost and confused, her world shattered. She lived like an orphan during this period, with her mother gone and her father unavailable and preoccupied with business.

One man who was a regular on the Los Angeles scene was Travis Richard Kleefeld, an actor and singer. Discovered by Dinah Shore, the American singer, actress and television personality, renowned as the top-charting female vocalist of the 1940s and with whom Carolyn played tennis, he performed as Tony Travis and was admired for his good looks, talents and charm. Born on 4th March 1926, in New York, he appeared in films such as *The Beatniks* (1960) and *The Fat Man: The Thirty-Two Friends of Gina Lardelli* (1959), and *Jamboree* (1957), and also made guest appearances in American television series, such as *Perry Mason* and *77 Sunset Strip*. In *The Beatniks*, he had the starring role as Eddy Crane, leader of a gang of small-time juvenile crooks, where his singing talents were utilized. As a singer, he was recorded by RCA Victor, a major American record label in the 1950s and he released several albums. Elvis Presley, of course, became the label's biggest star.

Before dating Carolyn, he had been engaged to actress Jane Wyman, who had been married to Ronald Reagan until their divorce in 1948. He was eleven years younger than her and it caused a bit of a stir in the gossip columns at the time. After his separation from Jane Wyman, he dated a succession of actresses including Debbie Reynolds, Joan Tyler and Sheila Connolly.

Also from a very privileged background, he and Carolyn courted and married in 1960 and soon had two daughters, Carla and Claudia. They were married for nine and a half years. Although Carolyn travelled to Europe with him, there were years of dissension. Their divorce was a crossroads moment for Carolyn.

Carolyn and Travis Kleefeld, actor and singer
© Carolyn Mary Kleefeld Collection

Carolyn says she was committed to giving her daughters everything she could— emotionally or otherwise—running the home, driving them everywhere daily, etc. until they reached about 11 and 12 years old, then her nerves wore out, as Travis was no support, and they were always fighting. She decided she needed to change things and talked with her girls to see if they wanted to live for a year with their father— they did. Carolyn's decision was criticised by a former boyfriend, who went on to marry the actress Doris Day.

Claudia and Carla Kleefeld
© Carolyn Mary Kleefeld Collection

Carolyn with her daughters, Claudia and Carla
© Carolyn Mary Kleefeld Collection

Carolyn made the decision to leave Beverly Hills and moved to Malibu in1974. She was in her late thirties. Her daughters were almost thirteen and twelve years old. She sought a different world from the mayhem of the social circles of artificial Beverly Hills. She wanted the clock of her life to tick in her own rhythms, more quietly, more spiritually. Having travelled the world, often pursued by kings and princes, she had done volunteer work to help autistic children and people in emergency situations and was on the board of the nation's largest Savings and Loan (her father's), as well as being on the board of several companies to assist doing philanthropic work, which has continued into the present.

Now she would begin to travel inward, the unmapped journey into the mind. A rented seaside bungalow on Malibu Road, with the ocean on its doorstep, was her first move towards a quieter existence. Carolyn wanted control of her life and time to explore her true selves. She began to taste freedom, a lifelong need of hers, in the relaxed and less demanding atmosphere of Malibu at the time. As she comments in an aphorism in her first book, *Climates of the Mind*, "one must transplant / when dwarfed and cramped, as a potted plant / your roots have outgrown their soil."

Carolyn and Travis's daughters would become highly accomplished women. Carla attended college at UCSC and received her Masters in Existential Phenomenological Therapeutic Psychology from Seattle University. She received her Doctorate in Clinical Depth Psychology from Pacifica Graduate Institute, and is licensed in NM and Washington States.

She became interested in Psychology initially around the ages 7-9 as her mother would take Carla with her to psychology lectures by Carl Faber at UCLA. Carla was a naturally curious, imaginative and relational child and was intuitive and associative in her thinking. She began reading C. G. Jung in high school. She was also naturally drawn to helping others and enjoyed counseling kids in her late teens and followed a spiritual, psychological and philosophical path forward. Carla has been working in the field of Psychology for over twenty years with numerous and diverse populations, working at several outpatient clinics, in private practice, and teaching at a Masters Graduate school in NM in Counseling.

She is most proud of directing an early childhood treatment center and offering play therapy to children ages 2—10, teaching as an Adjunct faculty at Southwestern College (Masters in Counseling and Art Therapy), where she has taught numerous

Graduate level courses. At the college, she has practiced with various ages, diverse cultures and populations. She has taught: Archetypal Psychology, Clinical Skills, Applied Theories of Development, and Psychopathology from a depth and relational perspective. She is also proud of her extensive training in Dreamtending, group psychotherapy, attachment and trauma at UCLA, as well as, related intensive mindfulness practices.

Carla thinks it is amazing that her mother has achieved such a level of literary scholarship and is so prolific in her creative achievements, and has published so many books both here in the USA and internationally. She feels the fact that her mother came from an immigrant family and grew up very much on her own, it is quite admirable that she found a path that has been most healing, transformative, as well as, immensely creative. For Carla, her mother has been a model of personal courage and a maverick in her dedication to her own mystical and spiritual journey and path.

This is Carolyn writing about watching Carla deliver her dissertation for her doctorate, "Watching Carla deliver her dissertation for her doctorate, I felt my daughter's nervous system in my very throat and was just short of tears. I was so proud of my daughter becoming the first doctor in the family, and of what it meant to go beyond the ancestry of oppressed females".

In one of her journal entries Carolyn suggests her daughter had "gone beyond generations of suicidal females" on her mother's side, "exhibiting the strength, courage, integrity, brilliance, and will to learn, progress, and be true to her higher nature. Carla is a living testament to what is possible in the individual—not just because of earning the Doctorate—that is a metaphor for the Greater Meaning of her Existence and of others. She exemplifies what is possible through deep, inner work, study and experience, and the value she places on that deep, spiritual awareness, process."

Writing about a visit she made to Carla's and Celeste Worl's home in Santa Fe, New Mexico's capital and a thriving home for the creative arts: Carolyn says "We had a truly magical evening with C and C—both at the studio—danced and sang and at their special atmosphere casa with its glowing Kevas and all my paintings everywhere. Celeste is quite the Magician with the music keyboard. (The) truly enigmatic flow inspiring the music got me going. Just what I needed. Carla made corn bread, hummus, feta, chili and greens. Just exactly my kind of food. Carla and Celeste's home is the only other home [where] I've been able to be truly comfortable."

Carla Kleefled © 2020 Carla Kleefeld

Claudia first went to Hampshire College six months after graduating at The Athenian School were she spent High School in Northern California. She stayed there for about a year and a half and then transferred to UCLA with her grandfather's support to make this change. She graduated from their art department with a BFA as a suma cum laude student two and a half years later. After UCLA she went to London to study painting at The Byam Shaw College and received a

37

graduate diploma from their program. She was supported to go by a family friend, Rita Pynoos, who was the wife of one of Mark Taper's partners Mr. Bob Pynoos. Rita was in the art world and spoke with a teacher and artist R. B. Kitaj for Claudia and his wife, Sandra Fisher, assisted Claudia to go to that College in London.

She began painting as a child and became committed and serious about her language as an artist when she was in College. She feels her main achievements as an artist are her inner journey and commitment to her symbology and truth. For her, the language of art and its process is very healing. Starting in her late teens and throughout her adult life, she has exhibited at museums and galleries.

Claudia is very happy that her mother has had an avenue for her language and expression and that she has remained committed to it for so long. She feels her mother's symbology and language have grown and sprouted into a beautiful thing.

Claudia's daughter, Chiara, was born in Taos, Mexico, in 2002. She pursued her acting skills at the Lee Strasberg Theatre, after her and her mother's move to Los Angeles when Chiara was four years old.

Chiara, whose acting name is Chiara Aurelia, is clearly committed to her art as well and her acting is her language as are other forms of expression. She is currently getting ready to graduate High School and loves school. She has also been dancing and singing throughout her time working as an actress. She became interested in being on stage at four years old and has remained committed to this art form. Her acting CV is very impressive and includes the popular American drama series *Pretty Little Liars* and feature films such a *Big Sky*. She was nominated and awarded Best Performance by a Young Actress in a Supporting Role for her role in the film *Back Roads* and in 2017 and 2018 for her role in the film *Gerald's Game* by The Young Entertainer's Awards as well as the BAM Awards.

Claudia and her daughter Chiara at Chiara's 16th Gatsby Birthday party in
New Orleans © 2018 Claudia Kleefeld

Travis Keefleld, their father, died on May 24th 2018. He is buried in Glendale,
California. Carolyn says he was upbeat and supportive until the day he departed.
Carolyn had a thoroughly complete verbal journey with Travis just two days before
he died.

PLATE 2

7. Carolyn with her father, Mark Taper. At her and Travis's wedding
© Carolyn Mary Kleefeld Collection

8. Carolyn
Photo: John Larson © Carolyn Mary Kleefeld Collection

9. Carolyn
Photo: John Larson © Carolyn Mary Kleefeld Collection

10. Carolyn in Tahiti with the girls
© Carolyn Mary Kleefeld Collection

11. Carolyn
Photo: Philip Fox © Carolyn Mary Kleefeld Collection

12. Carolyn
Photo: Bill Melamed © Carolyn Mary Kleefeld Collection

Chapter 4

MALIBU: FINDING HER VOICE AND HER VOCATION

"When I set out to find self, I created someone, I discovered someone beyond my imagination. So in losing self, I found my essence."

—*Carolyn Mary Kleefeld*

"May we live in a perpetual state of reinvention."

—*Carolyn Mary Kleefeld*

A thriving community of creative pioneers, including actors, musicians, and scientists, Malibu in the 1970s was a magnet attracting an array of unconventional people, interested in exploring the spiritual aspects of existence and journeying into the caverns of their own personalities.

North West of Los Angeles, Malibu is a city renowned for its image of representing the quintessential California beach life, especially surfing. Its rural beauty, with ocean and canyons was the perfect landscape for those wishing to be close enough to Downtown Los Angeles, which is thirty miles away, but sufficiently distant enough from the conventional throng and beehive busyness of the city. For these reasons, it is the place where many A-list celebrities, such as Richard Gere and Barbra Streisand, make their home. In the 1970s the Malibu Colony was the partying place of many rock stars. Actors Shirley MacClaine and Rod Steiger lived down the road from Carolyn's home.

Bob Dylan, a favourite singer-songwriter of Carolyn's, had a recording studio there nearby at the time. To the north of the Colony, situated in central Malibu, is Pepperdine University, a private college affiliated with the Church of Christ, where Carolyn would have a retrospective exhibition of her art in 2008.

For three years, Carolyn attended UCLA (University of California, Los Angeles), a university farther south, studying psychology, poetry, and painting. Founded in 1919, UCLA is a public research university and its Latin motto translates into "Let there be light". The legendary actor James Dean did drama at the university in the 1950s; and the singer Jim Morrison of The Doors became increasingly interested in poetry there in the 1960s.

However, the adult Carolyn, like the schoolgirl Carolyn, found it difficult to fit into the tight frame of organized education. Her spirit was too much of an untamed horse. Carolyn wanted, though, to increase the foundation of her formal knowledge and so she started to take continuing education courses in psychology via the UCLA Extension Program, now one of the largest and most comprehensive programs in the USA. Her teacher was the remarkable Dr. Carl Faber, who was brilliant at his subject and inspiring in his ideas. For her, he was her "first mentor" and a "poet-shaman".

Dr. Carl Faber, psychologist, lecturer, and poet of UCLA
© Copyright unknown

A professor at UCLA and its Extension Program in the late 1960s and early 1970s, Faber was a charismatic psychologist and also a poet, who had studied at the Jung Institute in Switzerland and was an author of poetry and prose publications. It was not unusual for admiring audiences of several hundreds to attend his lectures. He widened the approach to psychological and philosophical issues in an original and thoroughly engaging way.

Human Psychology was one of the forces shaping the minds of many progressives during the 1970s. Also known as Third Force Psychology, it was a different road than the limited ideologies of Austrian Sigmund Freud's Psychoanalysis, which offered a clinical method for treating psychopathology via dialogue between a psychoanalyst and a patient, and American B. F. Skinner's controversial Behaviorism, a theory that assumes behavior is a consequence of environmental histories of reinforcement. Human Psychology took the existential philosophies of Danish philosopher Søren Kierkegaard and French philosopher Jean-Paul Sartre further, considering the whole person as a lively, operating organism, rather than spotlighting parts of the personality. The holistic method of Swiss psychiatrist and psychoanalyst Carl G. Jung was a major influence. Jung instigated a holistic method and believed in "integration", that there should be a balance of conflicting forces within a person. Human Psychology's concerns with such things as individuation, death, loneliness, freedom, and meaning echoed throughout American culture. Faber's beliefs and teachings reflected the cultural happening. These themes would also resonate in the life and works of Carolyn, the artist and poet. Faber, in fact, would eventually write the Foreword to Carolyn's 1979 book *Climates of the Mind* and her 1982 book *Satan Sleeps with the Holy*. He also read her poetry to over two hundred of his students.

Another pivotal influence and inspiration at UCLA was Fred Gavlin, a prominent UCLA poetry professor, who took a liking to Carolyn's work. One day, he dropped to his knees by her desk in front of the large class, and looking up at Carolyn with tears in his eyes, pleaded, "It's just as important that you become a poet as it was that Picasso become a painter." His passionate outcry, his reflection of her as a poet left a deep impression, as she had not experienced that kind of artistic mirroring and inspiration having grown up in a materialistic environment. So in terms of creative encouragement, this was clearly a pivotal experience for Carolyn, especially later, when she questioned what it meant to be a poet in this world of digitized mentalities and market-place realities.

The move to Malibu was the real beginning of Carolyn acquiring the spiritual, philosophical, and intellectual motivation to pursue what would become her own distinct vision and dedication to her daily creative vocation. With Carolyn's children Carla and Claudia in the care of Travis, her ex-husband, for a year and Carolyn having the girls on weekends, she settled into her new life in Malibu. She would carry out intensive work on self awareness and the inner process of waiting for 'the ringing in the silence', to quote the German poet Rainer Maria Rilke, who would become a favourite of hers. Malibu, with its laid back ambience and its attraction for other like-minded truth-searchers, was also the ideal place for Carolyn to seriously engage with her self-educating pursuits. She was starting to come out of her Beverly Hills self-imposed "sleep". She was reassessing her life and confronting emotional realizations. As she was to eventually write in her poem 'Courage', "I refused the circus / now I walk my own tight rope / outside the massive tent". And: "I belonged to those who didn't know me and / I could not claim a self, myself until / I walked my own tightrope."

She needed to find herself, as she expresses directly and concisely in the poem 'Vacancy', which appeared in her first book, *Climates of the Mind*:

> *i have*
> *window eyes with vacancy signs*
> *mere mists of me drift*
> *behind my curtains*
> *no one is welcome*
> *i'm not home*
> *can others see there's no occupancy*
> *until i find me*
> *to return*
> *behind the windows of my eyes*

Her poet's soul was rejecting the glamour girl world and the price of so many years because she was not in alignment with her own essence, as she points out in the poem 'My Sister, the Moon':

> *I was returning*
> *to the city*
> *far*

48

below me
with its obscene mask
of facetious lights
no part of me was there
not in one light
or
shadow
I was alone in the skies
with a heart
so
anchored
with
hurt
it left no space for me

She spent the next years, until 1979, writing, reading, having some solitude, and also still seeing her daughters on weekends and weekdays. During that time she dated various men. Before moving to Malibu, she had met and dated Bill Melamed who had a profound effect on her re-connecting with the creative talents of her early years. She was madly in love with Bill but did not want to marry him. She didn't trust his stability.

The fact that she was surrounded by individuals who were ground-breaking in their approach to their subjects was inspiring. Dr. John C. Lilly was a good friend. Lilly was a medical doctor, psychologist and scientist who was at the forefront of research into the intelligence of dolphins. He also invented the sensory deprivation tank. His books include *The Deep Self* and *The Mind of the Dolphin*. His reading of Aldous Huxley's *Brave New World* in 1934 encouraged him to abandon his study of physics and focus on biology. In the 1960s, he carried out experiments with psychedelic drugs, such as LSD, in his exploration of human consciousness. Carolyn and a boyfriend went to Mexico to interview him about extra-terrestrials.

Another friend was actor Rod Steiger, the star of such films as *Doctor Zhivago* (1965) and *In the Heat of the Night* (1967), for which he was awarded the Academy Award for Best Actor. Carolyn and he dated and became very close. He was teaching Method Acting classes and Carolyn observed his diligent commitment to the belief that creating "artistic truth" must come from the dramas of life itself. She had, in fact, met Rod Steiger many years before they dated, at a friend's party, and he was then with his wife, the actress Claire Bloom.

She also dated Jean-Pierre Hallet, the Belgian ethnologist, naturalist, and humanitarian, well known for his extensive work with the Efé pygmies of the Ituri Rainforest, located in the Ituri Province of northeastern Democratic Republic of the Congo formerly called Zaire. He stayed at her Malibu bungalow. Carolyn was blessed with the range of talented and inspiring people she got to know and their influences undoubtedly seeped into her thought processes and added to her birthing as an artist and poet.

The 1960s in America spawned a generation that saw obvious cracks in the perfect American Dream. The technological machinery, advanced by the heavily funded world of scientists, was increasingly the man-made life force of a growing materialism. Ecological concerns fell into second place, some would say to the bottom of the ladder, when it came to the financial profits of large organizations. The Vietnam War and the ever-present fear of atomic war dented the innocence of many. There were movements desiring a more simpler way of life, a spreading interest in the spiritualism of Eastern religions and ancient philosophy, among intellectuals, writers, artists, free thinkers, and even other scientists who disagreed with some of the advances made by their counterparts.

Sexual liberation, popular music, and experimenting with drugs, such as LSD (Lysergic acid diethylamide), also known as acid were part of the journey that took young people away from the fixed safety and security of their parents' moral order. The Haight-Ashbury district of San Francisco became a mecca for young people liberated by the protest songs of the age, in particular those of Bob Dylan, the walls of taboo being pushed down in the arts and in literature, and the crowd chants of "Make love, not war".

One of the first major outdoor rock festivals was the Monterey International Pop Festival, which took place in 1967. Many young people were taking to heart the advice of Dr. Timothy Leary, the psychologist and writer, to "Turn on, Tune in, drop out". Timothy Leary and the Beats poet Allen Ginsberg, who was 'Oz' (Oscar) Janiger's nephew, both of whom would become close friends of Carolyn, participated in the Human Be-In event in San Francisco's Golden Gate Park Polo fields on January 14th 1967. It was the build up to San Francisco's Summer of Love for the so-called "hippies", "flower children", in that same year, which was attended by 100,000 people. The Woodstock Festival, which took place on a dairy farm in the Catskills in New York State in August 1969, boasted an attendance of over 400,000 people. It was three days, extended to four days, of "peace and music".

The period, though, was not a total revolution of love and non-violence. Protests with regard to civil rights, women's rights and gay rights often descended into violence to achieve their aims; and the Vietnam War was the backdrop shadow to the vibrant counter-culture of the 1960s.

By the 1970s, Malibu was home to many free thinkers who had experienced the 1960s and the sea-change of opinion on where modern America was going, indeed where Western societies were going. Malibu Canyon had, in fact, itself been the setting for the 1968 Easter Sunday Love-In, a celebration of the counter-culture movement sweeping across America.

So this was the America where Carolyn was trying to discover herself and her creative voice. It was an America totally unlike the country that had greeted her and her parents and siblings on their arrival as immigrants decades before. No writer comes out of a vacuum and Carolyn was tuned in very much to the different new voices born out of the discontentment with conventional society and its well-oiled engine of progress at all costs.

During her time in Malibu and among the alternatives offered by those rebel minds, though only Carl Faber really influenced her, she began to seriously express herself via poetry. As she would eventually write in a poem in her book *The Alchemy of Possibility*:

> *And I,*
> *with my pen,*
> *live the pulse,*
> *weave its patterns*
> *upon the page*

After meeting Anaïs Nin at the International Language Institute in West LA, they began a written correspondence. Nin gave Carolyn important advice, which included telling the promising poet to "find her own voice". Anaïs Nin (1903–1977) was a French-born memorist and essayist who was a prominent figure on the literary scenes of 1930s' Paris and New York. She financially supported Henry Miller for ten years when he was a struggling, unpublished middle-aged writer. They carried on a longtime affair. Miller, in fact, settled in Big Sur in 1944, where Carolyn would eventually settle. Carolyn visited Anaïs once at her home, and many years later, she attended her funeral wake. Correspondence letters between Nin and Carolyn were housed at the Henry Miller Library in Big Sur, until they were somehow lost. She later recalled in her one of her journals: "It fascinates me that I knew Anaïs. It seems appropriate that her writing, particularly so many years ago (maybe 35 years ago) had been inspirational when I was more influenced by psychological concepts."

Carolyn's poems were initially written for herself, but encouraged by the positive responses of others, she thought of publication, and Climates of the Mind, her first book of poetry, was published in 1979.

Carolyn with the manuscript of *Climates of the Mind*
© Carolyn Mary Kleefeld Collection

As Michael Zakian wrote in *Carolyn Mary Kleefeld/Visions from Big Sur*, published in 2008, the title was chosen very carefully, "The title outlines a key theme in Kleefeld's worldview. The mind does not stand apart from nature but is a reflection of the natural forces. As the body is subject to changing temperatures and climates, the imagination also generates its own environments and creates new worlds."

Carolyn with a copy of her first book, *Climates of the Mind*, in Malibu
© Carolyn Mary Kleefeld Collection

This is not too far away from the notion that Dylan Thomas expressed in his poem 'The force that through the green fuse drives the flower', one of his many anthems to pantheism:

> *The force that through the green fuse*
> *Drives the flower,*
> *Drives my green age.*
> *That blasts the roots of trees*
> *Is my destroyer.* [1]

Like the young but mature-minded Dylan, who was still in his teens when he wrote the poem, Carolyn in her first book of poems was displaying an impressive notion and profound thoughts.

With a very striking black and white portrait of Carolyn in half-shadow on the front cover and a Foreword by famous psychologist Carl A. Faber, *Climates of the Mind* is divided into six chapters, ranging from Chapter of Pantheists to Chapter of Spleen. As Patricia Karahan later Patricia Holt, states in her 'By Way of an Introduction', "Your odyssey, and therefore much of your writing, is powered by a sense of disconnection underlaid by your inherent belief in a truth which transcends the spiritual destruction you see around you." It should be pointed out at this stage that Patricia is essential in bringing Carolyn's work to the world.

That "inherent belief in a truth" and awareness of "spiritual destruction" would remain a potent theme in all the creative works to come in the following decades.

In the first collection we also see her already deep connection with raw nature:

> *Nature is the universal womb*
> *Totality   God*
> *All that lives, propagates within*
> *this self-generating circle of conception.*

And her need for aloneness even then:

> *Seclusion insists on my presence*
> *for my spiritual survival.*

That "seclusion" is also necessary for, and feeds, the sacred solitary act of creativity:

> *writing revives my dignity.*

The ex-socialite girl was shedding her old selves and finding expression of essence through her poetry.

Climates of the Mind, 240 pages of poems and aphoristic thoughts, covers a wide-range of emotional explorations. One senses a poet finding her poetical voice, a voice strengthened by her honesty and the vulnerable rawness of her heart's truths. The typographic layout used in some of the poems heightens the impact of her controlled and effective use of language, indeed individual words.

Before long, *Climates of the Mind* became a bestseller. Translated into Braille by the Library of Congress, *Climates of the Mind* has also been used at universities in human potential courses and at healing centers throughout the world. It is a remarkable achievement for a poet's first book. As Carl A. Faber points out in his Foreword to the book: "Here is a rare wedding of poetry, philosophy, and psychological awareness, without the self-consciousness of most modern psychological writing." A few years later, her book *Satan Sleeps with the Holy: Word Paintings* (1982) followed. She promoted both books by giving readings across the country between 1979–1985.

The astute business mind of Carolyn's father, Mark Taper, found it hard to walk over a mental bridge to understand the literary and artistic creative mind of his daughter. As English poet W. H. Auden implied in his poem 'In Memory of W. B. Yeats', "For poetry makes nothing happen: it survives / In the valley of its making where executives / Would never tamper". The valley of their differences separated them mentally, but in time, he would express his pride in his daughter's achievements as a poet and an artist.[2] Carolyn, in fact, would temporarily leave Big Sur and her love affair with John Larson, to be there for her 'Pops' in his ailing years.

After the completion of her first book of poetry, Carolyn became a participant in a workshop at the Esalen Institute, a retreat center and intentional community in Big Sur. The Esalen Institute was the brainchild of psychologists and ex-Stanford University graduates, Michael Murphy and Richard Price. It was their invitation to Alan Watts, an English scholar and teacher of Zen Buddhism, to deliver lectures that made a far-reaching impact on the organization they had founded in 1962 and who became a major cultural influence. Aldous Huxley, an English novelist and philosopher, along with his wife, musician and author Laura, made frequent visits and gave weekend seminars. A phrase coined by Huxley, "Human Potentialities" became very popular.

The Institute made a major contribution to the Human Potential Movement of the 1960s. The center was the home for the ideals of the New Age Movement, focusing on such things as spirituality, psychology, yoga, and personal growth. The two entertaining founders wanted a center for learning and development that would be outside the academic restrictions of traditional education. During the Sixties, the center hosted seven 'Big Sur Folk Festivals', featuring singers such as Bob Dylan and Joan Baez; and poets, such as Beat poet Allen Ginsberg, who later would communicate valuable feedback to Carolyn on her book *The Alchemy of Possibility*, and fellow Beat poet and artist Lawrence Ferlinghetti, who carried out poetry readings and workshops at Esalen. The center, though, remains renowned as the 'think-tank' for alternative and progressive ideas and beliefs.

The indigenous people of the area were the Esselen Indians, thus the chosen name of Esalen. The philosophy of the Institute was that there were areas of the mind and spirit that remained uncharted and thus unused. Nature could be one of the guides towards a deeper spirituality.

Whilst in Big Sur, Carolyn experienced what others had before her: the sheer impact of the stunning landscape of Big Sur on one's mind, heart and soul. It provides nature at its most raw state, its disarming beauty and, to quote again a phrase used by Alfred Lord Tennyson, the English poet, "nature, red in tooth and claw".

In Carolyn's personal and, for her, necessary pursuit of creative truths, her inward journey, she would take an outward step that would undeniably be a major factor in her becoming an established poet and artist, one whose works would travel across the globe. In 1980, Carolyn moved away from Malibu, whilst following her intuition, to her new home in Big Sur. Although she was not really aware of what she was doing, as she was then and still is an experimenter in living and in art, yet always intuitively guided.

Chapter 5

BIG SUR: VISIONARY ARTIST AND POET

✧

"The land of Big Sur is an infinite land, speaking of Nature's Untamable Forces. And speaking of the power within all that are One with its eternal laws."
—Carolyn Mary Kleefeld

"The unconditioned, the platonic rhythms, lyrics of life are offered to me on this mountaintop, this kingdom by the sea."
—Carolyn Mary Kleefeld

Big Sur © 2018 Peter Thabit Jones

Sprawling out its physical poetry and primitive allure between Carmel-by-the-Sea, a small beach city on the Monterey Peninsula, and San Simeon, a town on the Pacific coast of San Luis Obispo County, Big Sur lies between the Santa Lucia Mountains to the east and the unfolding Pacific Ocean to the west. Originally called "el pais grande del sur" by the Spanish, the big country of the south, the 90-mile stretch of Big Sur located along Highway One, is a fabulous natural advertisement for California's central coast.

The indigenous peoples, American Native Indians—the Ohlone, Esselen and Salinan tribes—were the first to settle there and utilise the resources of land and sea before the coming of the white man.

Today, Big Sur attracts millions of tourists to its miles and miles of majestic terrain, such as those wishing to camp, hike, explore by bike, surf, and those wanting to spiritually revive themselves in the natural world. Apart from the holiday seasons and national holiday snakes of tourist vehicles on Highway One and the accompanying packed parks and beaches, it remains a virtually untamed and untouched sparsely populated area.

Big Sur © 2018 Peter Thabit Jones

At the end of 1980, Philip Fox brought Carolyn to stay at the Ventana Inn, which comprises 243 acres off the Pacific Coast Highway and is half a mile from Pfeiffer State Park. A mountain resort, it offered Carolyn the opportunity to experience the more organic and lyrical life of undulating meadows and the silent and secretive kinship of redwood forests. She later bought a property in Big Sur on the top of a mountain, where she has lived and worked as a poet and artist for over forty years. Carolyn and Philip, whom Carolyn had known since the 1970s, had been married before coming to Big Sur, but the marriage ended in divorce after a short time. It was Carolyn's third marriage.

Carolyn's home in Big Sur to is situated on an isolated steep cliff, which slants its long way down to the mesmerizing swell of the Pacific Ocean. The property, 500 feet above the sea, has a 300-degree view from every angle. Her "dragon's crown", as she lovingly calls her part of the mountain, depending on nature's mood, offers the silence of paradise and the aggressive and wild music of the sea and ferocious winds. Fog can descend at any time and like the chilled breath of a god, submerge all in its cloud of damp and eerie smoke. In the summer, when the fog does lift, it can get as hot as a desert rock and one goes about one's day in a sluggish and uncomfortable manner. During the winter and even earlier, the anger of the winds is amplified and accelerated and they bully the whole place relentlessly. As Carolyn would write in her poem 'The Squall', published in her book *Vagabond Dawns*:

> *The icy grip of winter*
> *wounds the hallowed air.*
> *And the wind wails like a baby*
> *Abandoned in the squall . . .*

The wind, though, can brutally claim any month of the year. This is Carolyn's observation from a June journal entry, focused in its exact sense-impressions, "The garden is quivering. The storm moves its pulse, trembling, rushing in the squall. My soul is in this compelled rush—a sense of quickened current—to the unknown. The air is icy and blowing carelessly all that is in the beast, the wake of the tempest. The seas are like a receptive, needy beast—await[ing] heaven's blood humbly, vast, and eternal. The moonstone veils drape the mountain range, softening in this touch. The tiniest daisy bares its petals to the rippling, bristling blasts. The horizon is blue with the storms hovering secrets, getting ready to become form. White, gauzy entities roam the mountain peaks and the agapanthus wag their serpent-budded heads, condescending to the storm, the wind, the call of Nature's insistence."

The seasonal shades of the weather and surrounding nature are ever-present in her journal entries over the years: "The crows visit and caw. There are no seabirds at the coves and seas below. An opalescence glimmers in the blue mist of air. The enigmatic climes change again and a hush falls over the dimmed garden in its quilted warmth. The seas roar below, unmotivated by their lack of verve, yet shimmering with iridescent blue in their calm splendor.

Agapanthus, the wild echium, narcissus, white daisies, and crawling white clematis sing the garden. What a relief to have spring in our midst, in our veins. The winter was quite mild after all, despite all the exaggerated defense about possible highway flooding and mudslides. That only happened once, along with only a few nights of treacherous windstorms. Ah, it is a relief to be on this side of winter."

These extreme opposites in nature appealed to the emerging seer-poet and artist in Carolyn. In her chosen seclusion, "far from the madding crowd" to quote English novelist and poet Thomas Hardy, the climates of Carolyn's mind could explore the climates of her new world. The travels through her mindscape were furnished, coloured, inspired and challenged by the landscape, physicality of a particular place, the ever-present calm prayer and unquiet lament of the ocean, and the glass-clear, star-powdered skies of eternity.

The island-like reality of this remote environment would seep into her very soul and become the emotional and philosophical palette for remarkable works of art and arresting and lyrical poems. The "normal reality", though, would be transformed into the mythical and the magical, like someone entering a portal to another dimension, into an extraordinary fable, a metaphorical wonderland of psychological caverns and infinite truths.

She calls her home "pankosmion", a Greek word meaning "a place of the whole universe" and as Carolyn says "where everything is", and when Carolyn settled in Big Sur, she was following in the footsteps of some renowned poets and writers who were also attracted by the exclusive spirit of the area. Pittsburgh-born poet Robinson Jeffers made his home in a small log cabin in Carmel-by-the-Sea in 1914. In 1919, he bought some land on Carmel Point and set about building Tor House, a stone cottage for his wife Una Jeffers and their twin sons. The following year, he began the construction of Hawk Tower, in Gothic style and made with large boulders, now a literary tourist attraction along with Tor House. Some of his poetic themes provided the enduring image of Big Sur as a perfect retreat.

He came up with the term *inhumanism*, a notion that humans are too selfish and unconcerned with regard to the "astonishing beauty of things". This would be a theme that Carolyn would corner time and time again, and in some of her prose writings, probe in a deeper way.

The New York-born writer Henry Miller resided in Big Sur from 1944 until 1962, and his friend Emil White eventually established the Henry Miller Library, which opened in 1981, in the cabin where Miller had lived. Henry Miller's memoir, *Big Sur and the Oranges of Hieronymus Bosch*, published in 1957, covers aspects of his life there. Over the years, Carolyn has been one of the leading poets to have performed at the Library, which has also presented the likes of American composer Philip Glass and ex-Beach Boy Al Jardine.

Another New York writer and artist, Lawrence Ferlinghetti, co-founder of the iconic City Lights Booksellers & Publishers in San Francisco, known for its association with the legendary Beats poetry movement and where some of Carolyn's books have been on sale, owned a cabin, on land he purchased in 1960, in Big Sur's Bixby Canyon. He encouraged Jack Kerouac, the famous "king" of the Beats, to stop there, in an attempt to deal with his alcoholism and inner demons. The result of his brief residency in the cabin was the 1962 novel, *Big Sur*.

Henry Miller wrote in *Big Sur and the Oranges of Hieronymus Bosch* that "One's destination is never a place but rather a new way of seeing things".[1]

Gradually, over the years, Carolyn was truly able to break free from the oppressive straitjacket of her privileged but emotionally and spiritually stifling Beverly Hills' upbringing. She had shaken off some of the familial and social chains in Malibu. In Big Sur, she would nurture her real freedom and solitude like two beloved plants.

Part of the large living-room in Carolyn's home where she paints and works
© 2018 Peter Thabit Jones

Carolyn had arrived in her new environment as someone who had already purposely stepped on to a road of self-discovery in Malibu. Like many women of her generation, she had witnessed the 1960s–70s American Feminist Movement demonstrate their case for equality on the streets and via the male-dominated outlets. Her own very talented mother, Amelia, had totally sacrificed her artistic talents to the needs of her highly successful husband and her children. Carolyn was determined that she would give herself over to poetry and art, thus justifying the sacrifices made by her mother and her female lineage. As she was to state in her exhibition book, *Visions from Big Sur*: "I also inherited a lineage of oppressed females on my mother's side, some of whom committed suicide. My mother's German mother was not allowed downstairs until her less attractive sisters were married. My mother's feeling of resignation in giving up her art career to have children had a profound effect on my resolve to live differently. I feel my drive for artistic expression is partially propelled by my mother, that I am in a sense liberating my female ancestors today from what they suffered yesterday."

Indeed, she has seen some of her own artworks acquired into the personal collections of iconic figures such as Timothy Leary, American psychologist and writer, Ted Turner, American media mogul, and Dr. Oscar Janiger, a emeritus

University of California Irvine psychiatrist and psychotherapist, and a beloved friend of Carolyn's.

Carolyn with Dr. Oscar Janiger © Carolyn Mary Kleefeld Collection

Though being a liberator of her female ancestors, as an avid reader of books, Carolyn has embraced over the years groundbreaking male painters and writers, such as William Blake, Vincent Van Gogh, Marc Chagall, Gustav Klimt, Pablo Picasso, Paul Klee, Herman Hesse, Fyodor Dostoevsky, Rainer Maria Rilke, D.H. Lawrence, Charles Baudelaire, Dylan Thomas, Nikos Kazantzakis, a particular favourite, Benjamin De Casseres, and Aldous Huxley. Even today, her personal library and her conversations with friends confirm that the inspiration of these painters and writers, literary and artistic rebels to their vocations and visions, remain essential to Carolyn. She also likes watching films starring actors Johnny Depp, James Franco, Joaquin Phoenix , Woody Allen, and Diane Keaton. During the pandemic quarantine, for inspiration, Carolyn listened to Dr. Wayne Dyer and Michael Meade on YouTube. She says Dr. Wayne Dyer as a mentor changed her life; and she adds that for inspiration about our collapsing world Michael Meade is unusually helpful.

Carolyn stated the following about living in Big Sur in the interview with her in the 1993 *Mavericks of the Mind: Conversations for the New Millennium*, a book which also features the iconic figures Timothy Leary, Allen Ginsberg, Laura Huxley, and Dr. John C. Lilly: "It has accelerated my internal journey, and simultaneously my art, to be in a place where I can create the space and time to let all that's possible happen. It's an enigmatic and challenging environment. It's been essential for me to be in the constant inspiration of nature, where I can be in a position to live my own natural rhythms, and define my own nature. Previously, I didn't have time to do so. Here I'm able to create a world where I can live in my imagination as much of the time as possible."[2]

Carolyn and some of the participants included in the *Mavericks of the Mind: Conversations for the New Millennium* book at UCLA
(University of California, Los Angeles), 1994
© Carolyn Mary Kleefeld Collection

She was living by the statement she would make in her 1998 book *The Alchemy of Possibility*: "May we metabolize the poetic as our reality." She would also observe nature at work, destructive as well as creative, as she observed in one of her journals entries, "The land is eroding everywhere at home. I see it on the forehead here. I see it parallel to the beach and sea cove. Everywhere and everything is in motion, at rest without pause, as I once said. And the quintessential calm and beauty of this day feeds my soul-spirit in a most primal and comforting way." She was also aware of the need for spiritual and physical renewal and her desire not to become stale and safe in her creative and reclusive way of living, "Life on the mountaintop is sublime grace and a sublime blessing; but I must not decay in complacency and shrink in my fortitude. New horizons must forever be emblazoned and I must draw them to me—not get fat on lassitude and old trophies." She states in the same journal entries, " I wonder why I live in such isolation on the mountaintop. Well, I say to myself, you are busy all the time with your projects. But what about the normal, everyday contact other people have? Why am I isolated from this blood contact? Too sensitive, not of the everyday mold, although I am drawn tonight to miss that, that connection with the neighborhood spirit they share."

She did and does make visits to Los Angeles, to see various friends, "I have just returned from the heat wave of Southern California and the Beverly Hills Hotel. The experiences there were varied and stimulating. I am left brimming over with the feelings, sensations of my eight-day excursion."

Her readjustment to her solitary life after the electricity of the city of Los Angeles can, though, take some time. She has mischievously referred to her artist's life refuge on the mountaintop as her monastery.

Carolyn did, though, work together with Daniel Ellsberg and Helen Caldicott on anti-nuclear efforts in the early 80s. Ellsberg was an American economist, political activist, and former United States military analyst, who was famous for releasing the *Pentagon Papers*, a top-secret Pentagon study of the U.S. government decision-making in relation to the Vietnam War, to *The New York Times, The Washington Post* and other newspapers. Caldicott was an Australian physician, author, and an anti-nuclear advocate. Daniel even stayed in the the small cabin, where Tiger Windwalker now resides, for two days while they were working together.

Another visitor to her home in Big Sur was the American poet Coleman Barks, the renowned and popular translator of Rumi, the 13th century Persian poet and Sufi mystic. Born and raised in Chattanooga, Tennessee, Barks has since translated more than a dozen volumes of Rumi's poetry, including The Illuminated Rumi (1997) and The Essential Rumi (1995). He performed in Carmel, giving an inspiring tribute to Rumi. Carolyn says Barks also gave an engaging reading. She invited Coleman to have a sabbatical at her beloved friend Edmund Kara's cabin. Edmund had recently passed away. Coleman resided there for about ten days and her and David Wayne Dunn, poet, artist, photographer, and musician, visited him a few times, and Carolyn and David read from their forthcoming books whilst in his company.Carolyn says Coleman seemed to be quite taken with her and David's work.

Most serious poets and artists have to find or establish a space conducive to the creative act, and Big Sur, along with her focused and carefully chosen reading, assisted Carolyn in her maturing as a writer *and* as an artist. It was in Big Sur in 1984 that she really committed herself to visual art, honing her natural drawing and painting skills, and her studying of art at UCLA, via all kinds of media. She worked with private teachers of art, Ronna Emmons and Mary Titus.

Ronna, known as a dynamic instructor, imparts the Expressionist style to many of her painting students. References to Ronna and Carolyn at work on a painting are recorded in Carolyn's journal writings, such as, "I threw some paint on a 48" by 60" and thought it was nothing, so [I] took it out to hose it off and found a landscape. I left it outside for now, as it was so wet [and] hard to get through the doorway. Then I did a little one with very heavy paint and glaze–like it. *Unfinished Void* looks good . . . Then I got ready for Ronna and painting. We did good work on '*The Grist of Passion*' and it's almost finished. I'm quite pleased with it—it's very primal and gristy and messy with limitation. The colors are perfect. R, very helpful and sweet."[3]

Carolyn and Ronna Emmons by the Big Sur River
© Carolyn Mary Kleefeld Collection

Carolyn would mature into a prolific and spellbinding artist, sometimes producing up to forty paintings a month. One can see the impact of the Big Sur landscape and the natural forces on Carolyn's acute senses in a painting, such as *The Pagan Mountains That I Live On*, which was painted in 1989. It is a stunning and volcanic vision, where the ancient mountain terrain and the erupting ocean meet. There is a dynamic lyricism to Carolyn's use of mixed media in this work: it bubbles with such energy. The viewer gets the turbulent spirit of the location, rather than the captured reality of the scene.

The Pagan Mountains That I Live On by Carolyn Mary Kleefeld
© 1989 Carolyn Mary Kleefeld   32" x 40" Mixed Media on Museum Board

Though as with all focused and inspired creativity, there can be a price, "I've noticed how much my painting takes out of me lately. There's a sense of heightened energy and even exultant moments, yet mixed with a burning destruction and following exhaustion—even when I paint for just a few hours."

Carolyn painting outside her home in Big Sur Photos: John Larson
© Carolyn Mary Kleefeld Collection

Carolyn in her garden
(Photo: Not known © Carolyn Mary Kleefeld Collection)

She set about exploring her new world like a castaway on an uninhabited island, storing imagery, ideas, emotions, and the regular rhythms of day and night, which would be filtered—with her developing knowledge of philosophy, psychology, science, and literature—into heart and soul materials that began a passionate period of startling poetic and artistic production.

She told author-beloved friend David Jay Brown, in a published interview, when asked about living in Big Sur, "Being a pantheist, I experience God as nature and as the interconnectedness of all living things. Therefore, the power of this wilderness is one with my soul and work. Also, since I live on a mountain cliff jutting out over the sea, I receive the full range of enigmatic climes—from weeks of obscuring fog, brutal winds, and storms, to the rapture of paradisiacal days. Naturally these dynamical forces and polarities find expression in my artwork, and often offer sacred wisdoms to be discovered and integrated."[4]

When one looks through the 2008 Exhibition Catalog, *Carolyn Mary Kleefeld/ Visions of Big Sur*, published by Pepperdine University to coincide with the exhibition of the same name at the university's Frederick R. Weisman Museum of Art, one is struck by the breadth and the depth of the works painted and drawn in the first full-scale overview of her visual art, which cover twenty-five years of Carolyn's output, from 1983 to 2008. As the late Michael Zakian states in his very perceptive Introduction to the catalog, "Kleefeld is a spiritual artist. Her concerns lie not with the material and worldly but with what lies within. She firmly believes in a transcendent reality which unifies and gives meaning to the phenomenal world. For her, this larger reality of the unseen is seen around us every day but is overlooked by most people."[5]

She has said her work ranges from romantic figurative to mythological to abstract. In an interview with Rebecca Hill and David Jay Brown, Carolyn said about her 'process' when painting, "Often I work with brushes of varying sizes and shapes in acrylics–solid, liquid, and iridescent–but I also work in oils, inks, gouaches, pens, and et cetera. The uniquely thickened texture you ask about may be from the use of a palette knife or simply from building up layers of paint with brushes as I work the painting into existence. I also employ a quick-drying linseed oil, sometimes mixed with color for shading, and that also creates a glossy surface.

At one time, during the late eighties and early nineties, when I was creating my cosmic abstract series, I worked solely without a brush, intuitively pouring liquid acrylics, sometimes adding gouaches. Then, pressing down on the canvas, I would use a kind of "aqua-puncture" to draw the paints together, letting the colors blend and form serendipitous shapes which would always surprise me, for they seemed to have a life of their own. I would then use rags or paper to soak up the excess. Sometimes it took days for them to dry and reveal their final forms.

I also enjoy the freedom and spontaneity of standing over a canvas and spraying or dropping colors onto a wet surface. When I work with a garden hose outside, I like to move the paint around with the velocity of the water's spray, as if it were a giant brush. I love watching the formations morph into patterns in a way I could never achieve with the purposeful strokes of a conventional brush.

Another artistic secret is that mobility can ignite my creativity, and I have sketched countless drawings as a passenger in the car. Drawing while on the phone can also be quite a Zen-like experiment as I speak with one part of my brain and draw from the other [the place of no-mind]. Because my artistic process is intuitive and unplanned, the primary "secret" is being receptive to the Tao, and then expressing the streams of energy that may arise from this meditative state."[6]

She has named Gustav Klimt, Pablo Picasso, Vincent Van Gogh, Marc Chagall, Gustave Moreau, Alexej Jawlensky, and David Wayne Dunn as her favourite artistic influences. Carolyn, as an artist, sought to walk a very different path to those commercial artists lauded in the city galleries, where an artist's achievement is measured by his or her popularity among the "art trophy" collectors looking for safe works for their homes, works they can brag about when giving dinner parties. As she would state, "What it takes to create the sacred can be quite different from what it takes to offer it." She is on record as saying, "More than ever, art has become a product rather than a creation. Most galleries only accept artists who can guarantee a certain roster of collectors, or artists who paint what other people want, rather than create from their inner process. The same is true for publishers and writers. What would have happened to Picasso if he had only painted for the marketplace? We wouldn't have had the inspiration of his incredibly original artwork, different from anything we have ever seen before."

Interestingly, this is what she has to say, in a very perceptive tone, about Andy Warhol in one of her journal entries. "We had a highly inspiring day seeing the

Warhol exhibit. I'm thankful to D (David Wayne Dunn, poet/artist and her partner at the time) for exposing him to me, although I had met him many years ago in Newport Beach at Joe Van Ronkel's. Andy was there at that dinner party, quiet in a strange kind of way, like a burned out light bulb, surrounded by younger attractive and vivacious male friends. The leading fashion designer Diane Freedland was also there—very dark-haired, scrawny, and authoritative. I remember making an attempt to speak to Andy, but no dialogue emerged. Well, I'm glad I was open today to seeing, experiencing more of him, his art—or shall I say "productions." Was he an artist or a reproducer? I think the latter, but that's not to say that he wasn't truly innovative in a media fashion. A very extroverted sensation type—opposite from me, who comes from within. And certainly most clever, technical, and a brilliant politician. A man made for his times, the crest of the wave. People were his art—inseparable." And in the same journal entries, "Warhol, because he was such an extreme opposite, made me think of many things. And I was truly amazed by the innovations of his eccentricity, the incredible diversification of the mediums he worked in, the music and the albums and the zipper on the album for the Rolling Stones, along with so many media gimmicks that were extremely clever and sensationalistic."

Carolyn is always alert to art and artists she comes across in galleries. This is a journal entry on one of her getaway breaks and a visit to the Norton Simon Museum, in Pasadena, northeast of downtown Los Angeles: "I got ready in a leisurely fashion. Then Evan [the friend and driver she uses when in LA], Ronna [her art teacher and friend], and I went to the Norton Simon downtown. What an experience. [The temperature] was in the 90's, so it felt glorious to be in the sculpture gardens with [the] Henry Moore's—the ponds and blossoming trees, waterfalls. I lay down on a stone and listened to the lyrical waters and simultaneously the density of the city traffic pounding all around me. I was particularly affected by the Henry Moore sculptures. The art in the museum resonated so perfectly with the splendorous gardens. *The Mulberry Tree* of Van Gogh's. The small pastels of nature which were by Degas. Picasso, again and again. Courbet, Renoir. The art was beauty beyond beauty and the gardens and ponds mirrored that beauty."

This is her response to the J. Paul Getty Museum, Los Angeles, on the same trip with Ronna: "Another truly enriching day. Evan or "Captain Fleece" picked us up. We drove to the Getty, saw the Irises, not a fav (I far prefer *The Mulberry Tree*). I became deeply involved with Corot's forests and quality of life and times in those rich colors and stillness. The other great art was so endowed with another time when beauty was lavishly depicted.

After a visit to an exhibition of Picasso's work at the De Young Museum in San Francisco's Golden Gate Park, she wrote this poem, which accurately captures his masculine and energetic genius:

Picasso Exhibit In San Francisco

Picasso, you have left your mark—
painting imagination's metaphors
with such brute force,
breaking all the rules
like an Earth giant, smashing
tradition and stale concept.

You crafted with the cunning
of a bestial sophisticate
the paintings the world so admires,
exhibiting a ruthless artistry.

You led like an extravagant giant
with your experiments, sublime.

Did you enjoy this strength,
this brute force?
Did it ever annihilate you
to be so bold,
so brilliant, so brute a force?

She has also commented on the possible future of art: "I presume there will still be a diversity of artists, including those propelled by spirit, and then artists who are those fueled more by technical or digitized methods, and artists who synthesize both elements, and more. Van Gogh spoke of letting the technical aspects arise from the organic flow of his creation, an approach which I prefer in my own work. The current acceleration of technology has certainly had an extreme impact on art and on our lives in general. In many ways, civilization has become more robotic, less personal, so it follows that the art arising from a de-sensitized and digitized technology will be more glitzy and sensationalized, more sterile and soulless than ever before."[7]

Carolyn in her garden © Carolyn Mary Kleefeld Collection

Carolyn, like the artists she admired, wanted to scratch away at the surface of reality, to reveal a truth or truths, and she was not bothered if the end result was not "picturesque" to viewers of her work. She was painting for herself, painting to add to and expand her understanding of this existence, with its shadows and shining. She wanted to see her innermost places reflected. Art is her most honest mission and mirror. Carolyn believes that "invisible guidance inspires all of my life, not just my creative work. 'Sublime intuition,' as Krishnamurti termed it, has been my primary source of guidance, directly orchestrating my life rhythms. We can also receive guidance from the magic we discover in the simplest things, like cloud patterns in the skies that seem to speak ineffably to our souls. From my perspective, the Unseen is running the show and the visible is only a glimpse of the infinite source, of its seething cauldron of entities and forces in ebb and flow. The Tao-'God' I term it now."[8]

Her poetry in Big Sur increasingly utilised the forces of nature on her doorstep, which became the under-song of her poethood. Already in her first book, *Climates of the Mind*, written while living in Malibu, she notes in the powerfully energetic and atmospheric poem, "Rainwalk on Stinson Beach," a beach in Marin County in

California, that " My spirit soars / as a kite without a tail / I wait to join / the seagulls in flight"; and in the second stanza, "I am reverent to this transcendental force." In the third stanza, she acknowledges, "The skies lightning /Ignites my electricities / I prance / cohesed in the eternal dance." Big Sur would bring her spirit even closer to its communion with "the eternal dance;" and she would celebrate her discoveries through prose as well as poetry.

The American writer James Dickey once referred to a poet's "memory bank", a reference to the knowledge a poet acquires during their reading of books on various subjects, such as philosophy or literature itself, which will seep into a poet's poems in a direct or indirect way. The "memory bank" can also be the poet's life experiences, their personal dramas, as W. B. Yeats intimated in "Out of the quarrel with ourselves we make poetry". Carolyn's passionate relationships and her travels throughout the world obviously also added to her "memory bank".[9]

As evident in the poems from *Climates of the Mind*, before settling in Big Sur, Carolyn had already gone through a process of questioning who she was as a person. She had burned some bridges to the "false selves" of her past life, in order to embark on the rest of her life, to see the meaningful bone beneath the deceiving flesh of the world. In the appropriately titled poem "Beginning" in the "Chapter of Metamorphosis" in *Climates of the Mind*, she admits "I know I will walk with hesitation / until I can fully live myself—with confidence" and "I have lived half of my life and / I am only just beginning."

In Big Sur, Carolyn would set out to explore the dragon-shaped mountain where her house is lodged. A landscape inhabited by deer, rabbits, raccoons, ground squirrels, skunks, bobcats, gray fox, coyotes, and mountain lions; and an ocean that is home to seals, dolphins, sea lions, otters, sharks, and whales. Bird life is abundant and includes hawks, eagles, kestrels, blue birds, orioles, condors, cormorants, and sandpipers. Lizards and snakes, ranging from gopher snakes to western rattlesnakes, add to one's sense of a diverse and impressive wildlife.

She had already acknowledged in her second book, *Satan Sleeps With the Holy*, published in 1979, in a line that recalls William Blake: "All of the universe is in one tree, one bird, one flower, one person."

Her physical and imaginative explorations would become the mulch for the growth of her poetic and artistic visions. The car journeys beyond her home would also confirm the humbling power of the coastal stretch of Big Sur:

> *Hugging the jeweled spine*
> *Of Highway One,*
> *we drive around the hairpin turns*
> *above the sea's seething brine.*
>
> *As the infinite darkness*
> *swallows our hearts,*
> *we are lost to*
> *the spirit of wilderness.*

She has said in an interview with David Jay Brown: "For me, the lyrical climes of Big Sur resonate with the mythology of ancient Greece, particularly on warm, balmy days. This powerful, mystical land continually infuses my being and my artwork. As the infinitely changing vistas stretch out before me, I feel at times that I am gazing into the very eyes of existence, into a conflux of eternities." She goes on to say in the interview, "this poem of mine best describes my relationship to Big Sur and its impact on me."

In the Wild Elements

> *It was there—*
> *in the wild elements,*
> *in the lawless, ebony darkness*
> *on the mountain top,*
> *when all of her was*
> *raw, naked, and exposed—*
> *that she found her true nature.*
>
> *It was there, in the Unmanifest*
> *that her spirit became enraptured.*
> *There is the sacred darkness,*
> *the holy flames awaited her.*
>
> *There, in the feral wilderness*
> *pulsed the rapture of her radiant song.*

And she would discover in the journeys into her mind that "the inner country is wild and inifinite."

During these years, Carolyn did public readings of her poetry and had many exhibitions of her paintings. Alongside the fire of her daily creativity, roughly from1991 to1993, she was also the healthcare provider for her father. She has stated that it meant major work as she was involved with attorneys, doctors, and research to help her father in setting up his nutritional program and working as a manager with his nurses. She had to leave John Larson and their love affair, but they continued as best friends. Living in Big Sur, she has also been involved in philanthropic support of the community, supporting the Henry Miller Library/ Gallery, the Big Sur Fire Brigade, the Big Sur Health Clinic, The Big Sur Library, and other general benefits for projects and people.

Carolyn and her father, Mark Taper © Carolyn Mary Kleefeld Collection

As her father's health began to suffer, Carolyn took to visiting him in Beverly Hills and caring for him. A loving bridge developed between them. The weakened god of a businessman showed her his more human side.

In Chapter 41 of her book *The Alchemy of Possibility*, she records: "There, in the sterile environment of a hospital, lies my eighty-nine-year-old father, reduced to bare survival. How sad and humbling to see a man with a tyrant's will unable to walk or feed himself."

And: "My father was not driven by the spiritual to ascend the Earthly. His power and fulfillment came from outer accomplishment, from his financial genius. Now, with his disintegration, perhaps serenity will be his. He has been relieved of his extreme survival drives, commencing when he was growing up in an English ghetto during World War II, contending with air raids, bombs and the responsibility of being father to his younger brothers and sister."

And this moving and humbling paragraph, "As we sit in his living room, the last of the sun's rays touches his silent gray hairs. There, at the end of the day, in his sunset, we are of the same light. The radiance is the feeling shared, the touching of hands, of souls, in our vulnerability. He is so dear, so fragile, yet his nature is ever strong in its drive to survive."

In The Seams Between Worlds

O dear father,
always so far away 'til now,
when the mouth of dawn
threatens to swallow
your dying flame —

Now in your last flicker,
your beams are freed, meeting me
in the seams between worlds
where I've always thrived,
where you never went 'til now.

As you wet your toes
in the waters of the unknown
where other dimensions exist,
where the freedoms that escaped
your life on earth, await,
I'll be with you, always.

A genius of a businessman, philanthropist, and humanitarian, Carolyn's father died of a heart attack on 15th December 1994, at his home in Beverly Hills. He was aged 92 years old. He was buried in the family mausoleum in Hillside Memorial Park, along with his wife, Amelia.

The memorial plaque to Mark Taper at Hillside Memorial Park
© 2018 Hillside Memorial Park

The Taper family mausoleum at Hillside Memorial Park
© 2018 Hillside Memorial Park

His legacy, via the Mark Taper Foundation, established in 1952, has contributed greatly to the arts and education. A gift to the Los Angeles Music Center resulted in a 750-seat theatre in the Center being named the Mark Taper Forum in 1967. The Amelia Taper Auditorium was named in honour of his wife in 2008. The S.

Mark Taper Life Science Botanical Garden is located on the Pierce College Campus in Woodland Hills in the San Fernando Valley. His funding also led to the first gallery for modern works at the Los Angeles County Museum of Art, a memorial to his wife. He was a major donor to UCLA. The S. Mark Taper Foundation Imaging Center, a division of Cedars-Sinai, in Los Angeles, offers a full range of imaging services for adults and children. Each year, almost 500,000 inpatient and outpatient exams and procedures are performed and interpreted at the center.

From 1990 to 1998 Carolyn was writing her *I Change*, which later became *The Alchemy of Possibility* and which turned into an enormous job involving countless revisions and several editors. The book was published in 1998. During these years, Carolyn did public readings of her poetry, promotional interviews, and many exhibits of her paintings.

The poet [and the artist] does not just need to learn the craft of their vocation and build up their "memory bank", they have to eventually come to terms, especially the poet, that their giving their life over to poetry often brings in few rewards, even from fellow poets. Thus many committed poets often question the necessity, indeed even the validity, of their chosen life's journey via the written word. Even a poet as diligent, dedicated, and established as Irish man W. B. Yeats admitted, "All things can tempt me from this craft of verse".[10]

So when the creative person does find a like-minded soul, someone who understands what they are trying to do in their work and someone who mirrors their serious approach to it, the discovery of such a person is truly a blessing from the gods. Edmund Kara, a fastidious Big Sur sculptor and Carolyn's neighbour, became such a blessing in Carolyn's life and she in his life. He became her second muse, Dr. Carl Faber being her first, and showed her what it meant to live in Big Sur. His far-reaching philosophy also informed her of the commercial side of the art world.

Chapter 6

AN IMPORTANT FRIENDSHIP

". . .he simply was of her blood in some essential way"
—Carolyn Mary Kleefeld

Carolyn and Edmund became close friends, bonded by their passionate creativity. They were fortunate in that they did not want or need to work within the safe and cosy parameters of the mainstream art world. Unifying nature, in all its glory, was the springboard of their unique visions.

Carolyn with Edmund Kara, Big Sur sculptor and her beloved friend
© Carolyn Mary Kleefeld Collection

Carolyn had already rubbed shoulders and become friends with iconic free-thinkers, such as Timothy Leary and Ted Turner, but her friendship with Edmund came when she was really discovering her own artistic and poetic voice in her new life in Big Sur and, more importantly, he was on her doorstep. His cliff-clinging cabin below was a leisurely walk from her secluded home.

Carolyn with Edmund Kara, Big Sur sculptor and her beloved friend
© Carolyn Mary Kleefeld Collection

David Wayne Dunn, poet and artist, Carolyn, and Edmund
at her BB Nest property, 1998
© Carolyn Mary Kleefeld Collection

It was Edmund who introduced Carolyn to the works of Benjamin De Casseres, American essayist, journalist, critic, and poet, who remains one of her favourite writers. He gave her a copy of De Casseres's *Chameleon: Book of Myselves*.

Born in New Jersey in 1925 into a Jewish family, Edmund Kara lived a fascinating life, which can more or less be divided into two parts: his time as a costume designer and his time as a reclusive sculptor. His father died when he was four, so the responsibility of raising and supporting Edmund and his four siblings, one brother and three sisters, became his mother's, Anna, who owned a grocery store.

Aged just twelve, he had an exhibition of his portraits at the public library in Roselle, New Jersey. His drawing talents led to him studying at the High Arts School in New Jersey. His passion for designing clothes was a reason for him to get involved in fashion design and fashion illustration for various advertising agencies. Then, thanks to some friends, he began designing clothes for Lena Horne (1917–2010), jazz singer and movie star.

With his younger sister, Diana, nicknamed Dinka, he set up his own label, to produce high-fashion dresses and clothes for celebrities, such as jazz singer and actress Peggy Lee (1920–2002). But he did not like being a businessman. After working on three films as a costume designer for Universal Studios, he earned sufficient money to travel for a while across America and to China, India, and Europe, sketching during his journeys. He returned to Los Angeles and worked on a film for Paramount Studios. During his time there, he started to sculpt, using discarded beach wood. He moved to Big Sur in 1962, twenty-eight years before Carolyn settled there, and eventually built his own cabin, situated precariously on a cliff overlooking the Pacific Ocean and below the steep mountainside from the property that Carolyn would eventually purchase.

Edmund Kara's derelict cabin, Big Sur © 2018 Peter Thabit Jones

Edmund Kara's cabin, Big Sur © 2018 Peter Thabit Jones

Edmund's Cabin by Carolyn Mary Kleefeld © 2010 Carolyn Mary Kleefeld
5.8" x 5.8" Colored and Metallic Pens on Archival Paper

Edmund moved to Big Sur in 1962, though he and some friends had visited the area before. He was seeking an isolated and creative life, as Carolyn eventually did. He would spend almost forty years carving his incredible wood sculptures, whilst turning his back on the art world in his "suburb of Atlantis" as he called his surroundings. He is most noted for his 'Phoenix Bird', which dominates the patio of Nepenthe Restaurant off Highway One, Big Sur, and his nude sculpture of actress Elizabeth Taylor, which featured in the Vincente Minnelli-directed 1965 film *The Sandpiper*, starring Taylor and Welsh actor Richard Burton.

Edmund Kara's famous *Phoenix* sculpture at the Nepenthe Restaurant, Big Sur
© 2018 Peter Thabit Jones

He once said to Carolyn that the American has to make everything he does for sale. He never did when it came to his sculptures, and Carolyn would not either when it came to her writings and paintings. Carolyn says Edmund and she did not look up to any idols. They were iconoclasts.

Edmund, after entering a hospice in Monterey, died of an incurable bladder cancer on 27th May 2001. He was the inspiration of many poems, prose pieces and paintings from Carolyn. Over the years, she has walked many times down to his cabin, where one can sense his presence as the Pacific Ocean recites its old and constant music. She would walk in bare feet to his cabin as if in prayer with his soul.

She wrote movingly of his illness and later his death: "Edmund's pain and suffering has been pulling on me within. My compassion has been devouring my heart. I'm aware I'm of little use to Edmund. David Dunn and I went to see him yesterday and there he lay. He said he wouldn't read, as he did daily, and then proceeded to read to us from the *New Yorker*, giving us a glimpse of what poetry had been chosen by this prestigious magazine.

"He said no one was interested in lyrical work these days. The poems he read from the *New Yorker* sounded pedantic and linear. Even in his dying he gave us what we could integrate and learn from. He knew, this Merlin of a man, what was in our underlying consciousness. And now today, the date my mother died, he went to the hospice in Monterey "for a few days", he said. It was part of their program that you receive their treatment for three days before admittance as a resident. It seemed odd to us that he'd choose to die in an unfamiliar environment when I'd offered a full-time nurse or nurses if he wanted to die at home. I'd have thought he would want his own seashell to let go in. Later I heard his quick and impersonal departure was in most ways elegant and most considerate.

"Now on Sunday, 27 May, two days after Edmund's dying, I rest with my lover on a different log in the tree cemetery by the flowing, singing river at the Pfeiffer Big Sur State Park, and where some energy was restored. My soul is still a graveyard with my missing of Edmund, but I let the soil of my suffering breathe and a few emerald shoots of Edmund's death in me begin to sprout.

"The sculpture Edmund carved of two hands, one above the other, says it for me. The hand above being representative of the Source, the Mystery, the God of all and now Edmund has joined the ascending hand. And I, as the hand hovering below, will ever be open to the Ultimate, knowing now Edmund's essence has rejoined the Tao-'God'.

"The words that come to me after seeing Edmund's bedroom loft for the first time in the fourteen years I had known him are: 'richly embroidered, sensuous, with the passionate fabric of a dark, cave-like soul, dark and deep—primordial'. There was more power in his sleeping chamber than I can remember encountering before, ever, in the material world.

"My soul joins my dark One of a brother in a union beyond where we have been, to our essence, to our differences and to our ultimate core. Raw, honest, direct, religious to the ultimate were his sleeping chambers and the walls of these two rooms. His room with a cot, open on one side to the morning sun, was small and very dark with walls covered in ancient Persian-like fabric, too dark and worn to really see, more to feel or sense. The second bedroom, which one got to by ladder, was the same dark cave but larger. Neither had windows, but they opened to his gallery-studio of sculptures, with John the Baptist's hand reaching the good-sized opening to a bedroom, which was accessed by ladder. Neither room had adornments or objects, just a plain, pleasant mattress and a few old chests of drawers.

"His sleeping cave felt like he was not there with a lover, or lovers, except for the Supreme Dedication, which reeked of power, suffocating the heavy, darkness dwelling there. The walls exuded a quiet energy and sensuality, permeated with Edmund's energies. And the gray seas were quiet and gray down below his wooden seashell, bowing to their human neighbor of thirty years, to their commune of so many years."

At one time, labouring day and night as a sculptor, Edmund brought the leftovers of trees to life in meticulously crafted sculptures that are visual rhythms of the wood. He had a respect and love for trees, in particular redwoods, the fellowship of tall gods always venerating the sky. Some of his Russian ancestors were wood-workers and cabinet-makers. Carolyn also has a deep love for trees and she stated in the same series of journals entries after Edmund's death, "Both she, Edmund and David Wayne Dunn, her lover, seemed possessed by trees. They all painted, sculpted and wrote poems inspired by them. No wonder Edmund fits that metaphoric form without effort. There was a great tree on the way up the earthen road, on the curve to their homes, a great cypress that she had named Edmund."

Trees in all shapes and sizes inhabit her chosen retreat. Whether she leaves or enters via her front door or her back door, she is greeted by a congregation of trees like silent watchers of her world. Trees figure in her poetry and in her paintings. As she states in 'Night', a poem included in her *Climates of the Mind* book:

Trees
> *stilled in wisdom*
> *breathe secrets of centuries*
> *in mystic silence*

And in an unpublished prose piece, "Trees are the green fountains of the earth. In their glorious breath, they form the seed rains of existence."

   Edmund's Tree Song was painted in the year of his death. The painting is one of Carolyn's heartfelt homages to her former sculptor neighbor on the mountain. It, along with other paintings by Carolyn, is in the permanent collection of the Carolyn Campagna Kleefeld Contemporary Art Museum.

Edmund's Tree Song by Carolyn Mary Kleefeld
© 2001 Carolyn Mary Kleefeld 12" x 16" Oil and Wax on Board

Both Carolyn and her beloved creative comrade, Edmund, would embrace English poet Edward Thomas's lines from his poem 'I never saw that land before', "I should use as the trees and birds /A language not to be betrayed'.[1]

Edmund never betrayed the language he explored in wood; and Carolyn has never betrayed the language she explores in her art and in her poetry. It was she who gave Edmund his only retrospective exhibition in 1990 in Gallerie Illuminati, which she opened in 1990 in Santa Monica, California. She has described owning the gallery as 'a horrid experience' and 'a fiasco on my energy', though she sold $250,000 of her paintings during her period of ownership. The gallery closed in 1992.

The Gallerie Illuminati in Santa Monica, California
© Carolyn Mary Kleefeld Collection

When talking to Carolyn about Edmund, one senses a mountain, a place, missing a special "brother-artist". Yet for her and for others, what he achieved slowly and more or less secretly from the public eye, as a sculptor, sometimes working up to fourteen hours a day on a sculpture for months on end, indeed his creative energy, is still present on that very mountain. Meanwhile, his cabin, bit by bit, succumbs to its unhurried but certain demise. Carolyn thinks of his deteriorating cabin as a testament to his life, the womb of his creations.

Carolyn has met many other talented and creative people in her life, but Edmund is special because he was there at the springtime of her blossoming into a devoted poet and artist. He was a living example of someone giving their life totally over to the creative act, someone as utterly assured about what they had to do to create as a shark cutting through the Pacific water. He was also fascinating company, full of stories and opinions, a man of the world who had 'abandoned' the world to religiously work at his craft. Carolyn believes in synchronicity, a concept first suggested by the Swiss psychiatrist and psychoanalyst Carl G. Jung, founder of analytical psychology, which puts forward the notion that events are meaningful coincidences if they occur with no causal relationship yet seem to be related. As Dr. Wayne Dyer reported, "There are no accidents".

It certainly was a synchronistic blessing when she decided to move to Big Sur, buy her property on the top of a cliff, and become a neighbor of Edmund Kara. His input into her life ever runs deep:

"David Wayne Dunn and I strolled down to the abandoned seashell that once was beloved Edmund's abode. The ocean held his essence, the changing, after-storm skies, the bejeweled pine trees—all spoke of his biblical self, of the elemental forces that were, are him. A wave of melancholia drifted through the caves of my soul. No matter how rich his fruits of death, no matter how deep the grief upon his departure, how wondrous it would be to have him here, next to me. Do we ever know how much our beloved ones mean, before their discarding of cocoon? How within my molecular being he was. He was an ancestor and the main orientation I had as an artist walking the earthen path of the Noble Mystery. He had been that Pilgrim, that guide of this odd life I had fallen into (so suitably). He had been and still was a vital muse, yet he'd never tried to be; he simply was of my blood in some essential way, beyond personalities or obvious facets of their altogether different traits.

"And there, over the eastern horizon clouded with storm clouds, appeared the moon of him, as powerful as the sun of him. How did he live here for thirty years, one with the elements, one with the wood he sculpted, as it came to him, as life came to him—both in his living and his art—all the same. A flowing, basically that regard

91

for the honesty of Nature if followed. Taoistic, Zen, the simple, most direct way of living the truth of one's inner guide, soul. Yes, a devoted kin of my soul.

"The ocean, the sleepless currents embraced the rocky shoreline below. The pines were silhouetted against a fading pink horizon. Surrounded by the elements of wild beauty, I absorbed the tidal chant; the music of existence seemed to inhale me in this pulsing splendor.

"He was doing a praise-worthy job of being here, I thought, as I lay on the faded, dark burgundy, velvet couch opposite where he had lain on his matching Louis the IV couch. He so filled me with himself that I suddenly realized he lived within me; his invisibility finally had bowed to the visible. They had become One. Both the personal and the Universal were undivided; they were the whole. The Eternal had transcended the finite."

Her loss of Edmund, her neighbor mentor and her beloved friend, went deep. She wrote in a journal entry: "Whatever true relationship I found here in this neighborhood went with Edmundo. He was worlds of a person, so no replacing is possible."

And her continuing visits to his cabin over the years, brought out her love for him: "I gaze at Edmundo's cabin, at the broken glass windows into his kitchen where he made us his famed lime tea. How his cabin speaks of the movement inherent in the Earth, in the Tao, within ourselves. Embrace the moment, in the Isness. When I passed E's cabin, I uttered to his essence within me: 'How I miss you—perhaps more than life itself—the richness of you, of our friendship, of our communes.' And in his death, the protean soul, that seminal spirit doesn't depart; he lives on in this environment, in every budding pine tree, in the hovering echium, which he hated, and certainly always in the sea. The pine trees around your property are studded with cones, verdant green. I've noticed pine cones are in my destiny, from my early youth roots in Santa Monica."

And this is an unpublished poem to her creative comrade:

For Edmundo

(in beloved memory of dear Edmundo)

On this Mediterranean day in Big Sur
blue skies bask in white heat.

They seem to ascend,
giving us more space
to dream of the illimitable.

I call in your essence,
dearest Edmundo, and ask if you are
still listening like you were
that morning when you visited me.

You answer me silently,
in the undulating waves
lapping beneath your redwood cabin—
in the offering of your memory,
the rich essence you still emanate
from the altar of my heart.

Peter Thabit Jones, the late John Larson, the late David Campagna, and Carolyn Mary Kleefeld at the Edmund Kara Retrospective 2016 in Sand City, California. © 2018 Peter Thabit Jones

Chapter 7

AMA (Atoms Mirror Atoms)

✧

"Atoms mirror atoms—
Magnetic pools of eternal eloquence
In fathomless silence
So speak" —*Carolyn Mary Kleefeld*

Atoms Mirror Atoms by Carolyn Mary Kleefeld
© 1990 Carolyn Mary Kleefeld 48" x 60" Mixed Media on Canvas

By the late Seventies, Carolyn had been amassing quite a collection of poems. Then, in the summer of 1978, she was invited to join her beloved friend Patricia

95

Karahan, later Holt, who after completing her second year of Law School at UCLA, was working at a public interest law firm in San Francisco and had rented a house in Sausalito. Sausalito, a city in Marin County, California, close to the northern end of the Golden Gate Bridge is a place where colourful houses cling to a wooded hillside and equally colourful houseboats create a visually intriquing water-based community. Singer-composer Otis Redding wrote his song *[Sitting On] The Dock of the Bay* whilst residing on a houseboat at Waldo Point, Sausalito, in 1967; and Sausalito Library has a permanent collection of spoken word audio cassettes by Alan Watts, the 20th-century British philosopher, whose work would become much admired by Carolyn and would much inspire her as she was also a TAOist.

Carolyn had started to think about a possible book of her poems and had brought a lot of her poetry, mainly loose sheets in no particular order, to Patricia's place. Each night, Carolyn and Patricia edited Carolyn's poems. They were excited by the work they were doing, the focused process of making Carolyn's poetry into an organized manuscript. During the days when Patricia was at work in the law firm, Carolyn would do more revising and rewriting of the poems, which she and Patricia would discuss at night. Patricia said she could see the placing of the poems into chapters, each chapter representing a particular theme in Carolyn's poetry. Carolyn named the planned book *Climates of the Mind*. A personal dream was coming true for her, the birth of Carolyn's first book was taking place.

Carolyn and Patricia Holt in Malibu © Carolyn Mary Kleefeld Collection

During that summer, as the book really began to take shape, Carolyn and Patricia began to think about a publisher. Whilst editing and arranging the poems one night, they sort of looked at each other and exclaimed, "Why don't we do it ourselves!" They did not really have a clue what to do but they took the brave step to publish it on their own. They were, in fact, following some of the great writers in literature who also self-published their first book, including William Blake, Walt Whitman, T. S. Eliot, and e.e cummings. Carolyn and Patricia started their own publishing company, The Horse and the Bird Press. They often joked that Carolyn was like a horse with a free-spirited and strong-earth alchemy, and that Patricia was like a bird with a flying-above-it-all air-alchemy.

They managed to find a woman to help them in a minor way with the design of the book, but they already had a strong vision of the way they wanted it to look. They decided to place poems on the pages according to the messages of the poems and to arrange line breaks in unusual ways to communicate meaning, etc. They located a printer in downtown San Francisco and opted to do a limited edition letterpress book, with each book signed and numbered by Carolyn, and 5,000 copies of a quality softbound edition. It was a real learning process for them. The beautiful, professional signed and numbered letterpress edition of 500 copies sold out (with one copy selling for $250 even though the list price was $30). And, the softbound edition is now in its fifth printing, having sold over twenty thousand copies.

This first book of Carolyn's was an impressive success. It was a best seller at B. Dalton Bookseller, The Bodhi Tree Bookstore, in Los Angeles and Malibu, and in many other stores. The latter was the major independent bookstore in LA at the time, renowned for its array of metaphysical and religious books. It was at the forefront of the counter-culture movement and its guest speakers included in addition to Carolyn, Laura Huxley, the late wife of Aldous Huxley, who would become a beloved friend of Carolyn's later on, and Deepak Chopra, a prominent figure in the New Age Movement.

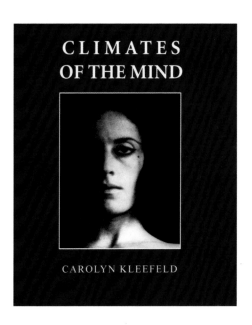

Carolyn's first book, *Climates of the Mind*
© 1979 Carolyn Mary Kleefeld Collection

Carolyn met Jacques Cousteau, the famous French explorer and conservationist, when flying home from Tahiti with her two children, Carla and Claudia. Cousteau drew pictures on the girls' arms, which pleased them so much. They didn't wash their arms for weeks. Cousteau then visited Carolyn at her home in Malibu. Carolyn and Patricia spoke to him about their publishing dreams and he said, "No one will understand what you are doing." He also told Carolyn and Patricia that they had been quite brave to start a publishing company with no knowledge of what to do and that he admired what they were accomplishing.

The book struck a chord with many of its readers and Carolyn and Patricia received many letters from individuals across America, saying such things as *Climates of the Mind* was like a life raft being thrown to someone drowning at sea. One person wrote to Carolyn and said it was the one book they insisted on having when they were in hospital. It was also translated into Braille, a remarkable achievement for an author's first book from a new publishing company. When it was first published, it was used at The International Educational Institute at Lindisfarne, which is associated to the Findhorn Foundation in Scotland.

The Horse and Bird Press went on to publish two more of Carolyn's books—*Satan Sleeps with the Holy: Word Paintings* (1982) and *Lovers in Evolution* (1983).

During this period, they received a number of manuscripts from writers looking for a publisher. One of the manuscripts was from David Wayne Dunn, a fellow American poet who had received a copy of Carolyn's *Satan Sleeps with the Holy: Word Paintings* from his sister-in-law as a gift and he was much inspired by Carolyn's poetry. After reading his manuscript, Patricia was drawn to David's poetry and wrote to him. She was inspired to give the manuscript to Carolyn who was also drawn to David's work and wrote to him. It would be the beginning of a forty-year relationship between all of them. After eighteen years of corresponding with Carolyn, she asked him in1998 to be a poet-in-residence in her cabin, "The Rainbow Room", below her home. A lovely synchronicity was present as David first wrote to Carolyn and Patricia on 8th April 1980 and he arrived to reside in the cabin on 8th April 1998. Soon after David arrived, he joined in a get-together Carolyn hosted for Laura Huxley, wife of Aldous, who was visiting Carolyn at the time before going to the Esalen Institute to present a seminar with Shangai-born philosopher and Tai Chi master Chungliang Al Huang. David, as we shall eventually see, became an important muse, painter, and lover to Carolyn and she to him as they inspired each other to push the boundaries of their artwork and their poetry.

Carolyn with David Wayne Dunn, American poet and artist
© Carolyn Mary Kleefeld

By 1980, Carolyn had made her home in Big Sur. Four years later Patricia had also made her home in Big Sur. By the end of 1984, they ended their publishing company, as it had become more of a business challenge than a creative endeavor. They still edited Carolyn's poetry together, but decided to find other publishers for her books. At that time, painting had become a more integral part of her creative life, and eventually Carolyn formed Atoms Mirror Atoms, Inc. to serve as an umbrella for her poetry and prose, which it does to this day.

The company name comes from the title of a poem by Carolyn and is also the title of a 1990/91 painting by Carolyn; and she had this to say about "atoms mirror atoms" in the 2008 *Visions from Big Sur* exhibition catalogue: "It expresses a poetic synthesis of some key principles of religion and physics: Every action has an equal and opposite reaction; what you sow so shall you reap; like not only attracts, but begets like." She also states: "When we contemplate the number of atoms in existence, we begin to glimpse the scope of life's mathematical equations. With the emergence of each atom, another is born, and with the diversification comes mutation, evolution's promise." And: "All we need to do is breathe, and atoms mirror atoms." Atoms for Carolyn is not just a scientific term, it is used by her in a Blakean way as a term on quantum for many things that are small, beloved, essential, and indicate a quantum reality.

Carolyn and Patricia have been working together with AMA for thirty years, though their friendship and working relationship goes back to forty-seven years. Carolyn comments on Patricia and their editing process time and time again in her journal entries. She is always aware of Patricia's indispensable skills and true devotion to their work together: "P's unbelievable kindness, the way she worked with me tonight with the last of the editing, is so touching. It is really enough in itself for me to have such a friend. Beyond lucky." And: "The editing went super well and easily. 'Kreetch' (Carolyn's nickname for Patricia) made incredible edits—supremely helped the book. We had a delightful time. Then we came up here and finished all her edits. She will take my book with her to finish. She is going to Washington on Thursday. I will miss not having her nearby. I've never felt as close. We are such sisters, as different as we are." This comment on Patricia was written three years after the other journal entries: "Her sacrificial, heroic, self-effacing devotion. She is truly amazing in her support and devotion of me, my work. Patricia is indispensable in birthing my life and work. How deeply fortunate I am. A great, ultimate blessing she is. A true angel."

Carolyn and Patricia © 1998 Carolyn Mary Kleefeld Collection

Carolyn, Patricia, and Needja © 2021 Tiger Windwalker

Kirtana, an internationally established singer-songwriter and guitarist of enchanting and beautiful songs, started working for Carolyn around 1987. Kirtana, who has performed her songs across the world, had answered an advertisement from AMA for an 'Art assistant'. Initially she worked just one day a week, ordering paint supplies, etc. Kirtana was also working four days a week at a craft gallery in Carmel at the time. In fact, the vocation of the artist was not new to Kirtana as she had grown up with a father who was a successful full-time artist. At the time of taking up the AMA job, she was living in Bixby Bridge Canyon, across the road from poet and artist Lawrence Ferlinghetti's cabin.

In addition to ordering art supplies, very early on she began cataloguing all of Carolyn's writing on that new-fangled invention just emerging back then called the "personal computer." As time went on, Carolyn would ask her to do other things, and work more hours, so gradually she became more of a "personal assistant." Within a few years, Kirtana was not only doing the usual kinds of personal assistant tasks, but managing the database of Carolyn's art. And at a later time, Kirtana digitized 40 years of Carolyn's personal journals for the archives at the Carolyn Campagna Kleefeld Contemporary Art Museum.

Carolyn and Kirtana © Carolyn Mary Kleefeld Collection

At a certain point Kirtana felt that she couldn't attend to her own growing music business and still keep Carolyn satisfied, so she quit. But she told Carolyn when she quit that if she ever wanted help just with her writing, she would enjoy doing that, especially if the work could be part-time with a flexible schedule (to support Kirtana's touring). Within about 6 months, Kirtana was working for Carolyn again—this time, just with Carolyn's writing. Kirtana loves playing with words and has from an early age. In fact she majored in English Literature with an emphasis on Creative Writing.

With regard to Carolyn's writing, when Kirtana began 30 years ago, she just recorded what she wrote verbatim. After all, as Kirtana says, Carolyn is an amazing writer and a published author, so Kirtana thought, who am I to suggest an edit? She also knew that Carolyn didn't really like re-working her writing; she favored the purity of her original stream of consciousness. But occasionally, Kirtana would suggest a very tiny change or ask permission to "clean" the writing up a bit. Over time, she got braver with her suggestions, and eventually Carolyn came to actually enjoy the editing process, much to her surprise. Because she has known Carolyn and the uniqueness of her vocabulary and style for so long, they have developed an unusual way of working together. Kirtana feels she doesn't really have an official title, except to say that she assists Carolyn with her writing. In addition to the recording and organizing all of Carolyn's written work, and the editing suggestions, Kirtana brings a kind of organizational coherence to the structure of Carolyn's writing and books. For example, as Carolyn points out, *The Alchemy of Possibility: Reinventing Your Personal Mythology* was organized from over a 1,000 pages to 56 chapters due to Kirtana's genius of organisation.

Carolyn says this about Kirtana in one of her journal entries, whom she refers to as WD (Wild Dove, Carolyn's pet name for Kirtana): "Being able to count on her, her golden patience, fairness, trustworthiness, honesty that I can send my journals and never have a thought about them not being treated with utter confidentiality. The incredible integrity of WD's editing work with me, not to forget her talents, which are many. I think she gives me what I didn't have growing up, that golden stability and dependability. She has kept me, my writing alive all these years. How can I ever thank her enough? Her soul feels as pure as one could ever meet. That too makes me weep. What a blessing you are, dearest WD. How proud I am of her success as a creator. How truly wonderful she is, internationally acclaimed–all through her gifts of being as an artist, musician, and person. I have such high regard and respect for her. Also, being an organizational genius she is ever thanked for putting *The Alchemy of Possibility* into 56 chapters."

This section from an interview with American writer David Jay Brown, a beloved friend of Carolyn's, perfectly illustrates how a book by Carolyn, in this case [in 1998] *The Alchemy of Possibility*, comes into being and the ripples it can make in the literary world: "*The Alchemy of Possibility* was derived from approximately a thousand pages of journals spanning ten years. During those years, I was most inspired by the *I Ching*. I didn't know when I was writing those journals that they would one day become a book; I was simply recording my life experiences at the time, out of an inner necessity.

"Kirtana, my beloved friend and editor, played the essential role of organizing those thousand pages by themes. We then thought of using the Tarot along with the *I Ching* and it began to take shape after a lengthy labor of love. The other cherished friend and editor, Patricia Holt, later assisted me in reviving some of the lost poetic essence after too many layers of editorial input from as many as five editors. Then I spent three months in sheer isolation at the BB Nest high up on the mountaintop completing the book. Allen Ginsberg also advised me, along with Laura Huxley, who was very encouraging of my work and wrote a most insightful and passionate Foreword.

"But then, just as the birth seemed imminent, brutal storms wreaked havoc, closing down the highway for months. So we had the added challenge of finding a way to get ourselves and the manuscript back and forth between Big Sur and Monterey, where our book designer and publisher had their offices. So some births are clearly more laborious than others, but eventually this love-child took form. In addition to becoming one of my bestselling books, *The Alchemy of Possibility* has been used as a textbook in art classes and healing centers around the world.

"When *The Alchemy of Possibility* was first published, I gave various readings around the country, and invited people to hold the book, allow a question to arise, and then open to a page at random. Remarkably and repeatedly, participants were amazed at the resonance, relevance, and illumination they received. These experiments helped validate the divination aspect of *Alchemy*.

"As a result, the website www.alchemyoracle.com was created by Richard Rasa, based entirely on the book and including all the text and images. At the Bodhi Tree, I saw the living example of it when Mytheos Holt (my godson) wildly exclaimed how right on the oracle was for him.

"Whether using the book or the online Oracle, the deeper psyche of the reader-participant is revealed, propelling the discovery of his or her own way. The insights derived from this kind of oracle emanate from each person's life process rather than from the projections of an authority figure.

Because my art and poetry are propelled from the same ancient wells, the magnetic fields that have existed primordially, we can resonate with them beyond our minds. It is from this place of oneness that we can intuit what we need to discover, letting the synchronicity of the moment guide our way."[1]

In June of 1997, Carolyn met American writer and sculptor John Dotson. John interviewed her and fellow poet-artist David Wayne Dunn about their book, *Indian Love,* at the Henry Miller Library, Big Sur, for a radio series. *Indian Love* was later published as *Kissing Darkness.* These recordings were done for KUSP in Santa Cruz, a community station where John was the producer and host. Carolyn had earlier sent a copy of *Climates of the Mind* to John who was the producer/host of *Ars Poetica?* on KAZU Monterey Bay Public Radio, a program that ran from 1984 to 1999. Subsequent programs John hosted were *One Place* and *Global Positioning,* until 2004. KAZU is an NPR-member radio station.

John Dotson © 2020 John Dotson

A special and inspiring friendship developed between Carolyn and John, who would do occasional work for AMA. Apart from his writings, one of them a much respected book on the Robinson Jeffers Tor House, and his original sculptures, John is an excellent organizer of literary/cultural events at the McGowan House in Monterey and events connected with the Monterey Peninsula Friends of C. G. Jung in the Carmel and Monterey areas. In 2007, John introduced Stanley H. Barkan, an internationally-published poet and renowned publisher, to Carolyn.

Stanley, who was born in 1936 and who grew up in Brooklyn, New York, founded, with the loyal support of his artist wife Bebe Barkan, the remarkable Cross-Cultural Communications publishing company in 1971; and poets Pablo Neruda, American Poet Laureate Stanley Kunitz, Allen Ginsberg, and novelist Isaac Asimov are among the many international authors he has published. In its 46 years of publishing, Cross-Cultural Communications, often referred to as CCC, has produced over 500 titles in over 60 different languages, which is an astonishing achievement for a publisher, especially one focusing primarily on poetry and translations of poetry. Stanley's and Bebe's Long Island, New York, home is the hub of CCC and it is always a hive of daily and nightly activity. CCC is the publisher of Carolyn's *Soul Seeds: Revelations and Drawings* in 2008 and *Vagabond Dawns* in 2009. CCC also co-published, with my The Seventh Quarry Press, which I founded in 2005, her books *Psyche of Mirrors: A Promenade of Portraits* (2012) and *The Divine Kiss: An Exhibit of Paintings and Poems in Honor of David Campagna* (2014).

Stanley has gone on to arrange and co-publish a number of her books in other languages with publishers in the respective countries. These include: *Vagabond Dawns* (Korean/English bilingual edition) Translated by Irene Seonjoo Yoon (2012) Korean Expatriate Literature/Cross-Cultural Communications; (2013); *Soul Seeds: Revelations and Drawings* (Korean/English bilingual edition) Translated by Dr. Byoung K. Park (2014) Korean Expatriate Literature/Cross-Cultural Communications; *Soul Seeds Revelations and Drawings* (Japanese/English bilingual edition) Translated by Naoshi Koriyama (2014) Coal Sack Publishing Company/Cross-Cultural Communications; *Soul Seeds: Revelations and Drawings* (Sicilian/Italian/English trilingual edition) Translated by Gaetano Cipolla, (2014) Legas Publishing. Stanley has arranged further bilingual books of her work, and they were published in Romanian, Bulgarian, Russian, Persian, Chinese, Catalan, and Spanish editions in 2019. Individual poems by Carolyn have been translated into Korean, Romanian, Japanese, Italian, Persian, Sicilian, Chinese, Arabic,

Bengali, Bulgarian, Russian, Greek and other languages.

Also, as a result of her ongoing collaboration with Dr. Olimpia Iacob, whom I introduced to Stanley and to Carolyn, after my two visits as a poet/lecturer to Romania, a Romanian/English bilingual edition of both *Vagabond Dawns* and *The Divine Kiss* have been published, in 2013 and 2014 respectively. Carolyn is ever grateful to Stanley for his devotion and his international promotion of her creative works.

Stanley H. Barkan, Carolyn's American publisher and fellow poet
© 2018 Mark Polyakov

Peter Thabit Jones, Carolyn, and their publisher Stanley H. Barkan in Big Sur
© 2018 Patricia Holt

With regard to Carolyn's artwork, it has appeared in numerous galleries and museums over the past 25 years. The Frederick R. Weisman Art Museum at Pepperdine University in Malibu, California, exhibited a retrospective of her paintings and drawings and published an exhibition catalogue, *Carolyn Mary Kleefeld: Visions from Big Sur*, with art from the exhibit and a commentary by museum curator and director, the late Michael Zakian, Ph.D. (2008).

Other major solo exhibitions include "30 years of Abstract Visions" at the Gallery at the Ventana Inn in Big Sur, California (2014), "The Divine Kiss" at the Karpeles Manuscript Library Museum in Santa Barbara, California (2013) and Shreveport, Louisiana (2014), "Art, Poetry, and Reflective Prose" at the Walter Lee Avery Gallery at the Seaside, California City Hall (2002), "Parallel Universes: Visions for the 21st Century" at the Stowitts Museum & Library in Pacific Grove, California (2001), "A Retrospective from Abstract to Neo- Impressionism" at the corporate offices of "333 Bush Street" in San Francisco, California (1999), and a poetry reading and art exhibit at Gallerie Illuminati in Santa Monica, California (1990).

Her art has also been exhibited at The American Jewish University, Los Angeles (2016), The B. J. Spoke Gallery, Huntington, New York (2014), The Old Courthouse Art Center, Woodstock, Illinois (2014), The New York Hall of Science, New York, NY (2013), the Alexandria Museum of Art, Alexandria, Louisiana (2013), Woman Made Gallery, Chicago, Illinois (2001), University of California Santa Cruz, Santa Cruz, California (2001) National Arts Club in New York, New York (2001), and Nassau County Museum of Art, Roslyn Harbor, New York, among others. It is in the permanent collections, among others, of The Downey Museum of Art, The Frederick R. Weisman Art Museum, The Henry Miller Memorial Library in Big Sur, and the Dylan Thomas Theatre in Swansea, Wales. In addition to being featured in art magazines, textbooks, and on the cover of poetry books, her art can be found in the personal collections of Ted Turner, the American media mogul and philanthropist, the estates of Laura Archera Huxley, Dr. Timothy Leary, and many others, as well as at the United Nations.

The Monterey Public Library Archive, California, has accepted Carolyn's archive of work in its California History Room at 625 Pacific Street in Monterey. All of her books are catalogued there, as well as book reviews, press releases, newspaper and magazine articles, etc. from 1979 when her first book, *Climates of the Mind*, was published, up through the present. Students and other patrons will have access to her work for their research and studies. The Museum of Modern Art in New York Archive has expanded their archive of her work, accepting her books which include her artwork, and book reviews, press releases, newspaper and magazine articles, etc., from 1991 with her solo exhibit at Gallerie Illuminati in Santa Monica, California, up through the present. Students and other patrons will have continuing access to her work for their research and studies. Letters by Carolyn sent to emeritus professor and poet Vince Clemente and some of her books and other materials are archived at the Vince Clemente Archive at Rochester University, New York. Also, see Chapter 12, which details the opening of the Carolyn Campagna Kleefeld Contemporary Art Museum in February 2022.

Her poetry is also studied, along with the writings of seven other acclaimed woman writers, such as Edna St. Vincent Millay, Maya Angelou, Maria Mazziotti Gillan, and Aeronwy Thomas, in a continuing course, "The Other Half of the Sky: Eight Women Writers," which I taught at Swansea University, Wales, UK, until my retirement in 2015. She is an Honorary Member of IMMAGINE&POESIA, the artistic literary movement founded in Turin, Italy, by Lidia Chiarelli and Gianpiero

Actis, under the patronage of the late Aeronwy Thomas, daughter of Dylan Thomas. She has appeared on the World Poetry Café Radio Show (Canada), hosted by Ariadne Sawyer. Carolyn and her AMA team can be justifiably proud of the international impact they have all made with her writings and her artwork.

Carolyn © Carolyn Mary Kleefeld Collection

Chapter 8

LOVE AS THE INSPIRATION

*"Why am I called to write about love, passion—the transcendence that
two loving souls can engender?"*
—*Carolyn Mary Kleefeld*

*"Falling in love implies sinking into the unconscious because we are
biochemically so drawn to another that our mind is, for those moments,
let go of like a wacky kite."*
—*Carolyn Mary Kleefeld*

*"I recognize you, my lover,
as one of my darling shadow-selves."*
—*Carolyn Mary Kleefeld*

Carolyn lived through the 1960s and the cultural explosion of "love" as a freeing power against the cold rigidity of materialism and its controlling forces. Love and her lovers have always been important inspirations for her poetry, other writings, and paintings. Being so sensitive to the lover in her life, her love poetry in particular runs the whole range of emotions, from the tender to the erotic. There are no boundaries to her deep feelings for the man in her life and the expression of him through her artworks and writings. As she points out in an unpublished work, *Rippling Revelations*, "It's been all about love. Love is IT, the ultimate force."

Apart from her first three husbands, several men have been all-important in Carolyn's life, namely Bill Melamed, John "Wolf" Larson, David Wayne Dunn, and her fourth husband, David Campagna, her ultimate love. Later, in the recent past, Dr. Arthur Williamson is her love muse.

After separating from her husband Travis, she entered into a relationship with Bill Melamed, whom she describes as a great love of hers. His family owned coast-to-coast stores in America. Bill and Carolyn flew to places such as the Caribbean in his private jet. He was a member of the Hillcrest Country Club, a private social club in Los Angeles. The actors and singers Danny Kaye and Al Jolson were among the famous members of the Club. According to Carolyn, Bill was like a poet in the social world, bombastic and someone who broke the rules of the Club. He would walk around the premises bare-footed and eating pecan pie. Russian-Jewish, he was very romantic towards Carolyn. She says her daughters loved him. He taught Carolyn to fly a plane, but she never flew one by herself. Born in 1935, he died in 1991. This poem captures the sheer energy he brought into her life:

You are a hurricane
You are the wind of my life
making me breathless
Blowing my hair here—there
not staying anywhere of me
long enough to know me
really know me
You move so fast in your currents
Excitement to touch—feel—
in seconds spread my pollen, honey
all over you
into your eager mouths
My currents blend into yours
our rhythms excite me
I am blown away from myself
out of control—lost within yours
      ah . . .

And this very tender and elegiac poem expresses Carolyn's feelings about Bill's mortal departure:

Song To My Dying Love

For William Melamed (1935-1991)
Poet of life, pilot, sportsman and businessman

Breathe, my dearest man,
breathe into the candle's light

112

Let your being drift
into the river's currents

Let yourself be that current
Let yourself go to current
Be the symphony of
your greatest dreams,
my darling man

Perhaps it is I
who is dying
in your leaving,
not you, who is
entering a new life

Bill continued to inspire Carolyn after his death. She never forgot that they had experienced new worlds together and he had helped her rediscover the child-poet inside.

For Bill Melamed

You returned my poetry to me
which had been lost
in growing up.

United with the passion
of your extravagance,
I re-found myself,
the child-poet who could soar
with you and beyond . . .

As in life,
so in your death
you inspire me
to write and feel.

She recalls in an entry in one of her journals, "Well, I saw a bunch of old photos—truly amazing. My eyes were so large. There was a photo of Bill Melamed gazing at me. He really looked young and handsome. And he is looking at me with urgency (very sexy). Heavens, that was before I changed my life–over thirty years

113

ago—and came to Big Sur. I was younger in those photos than my daughters are now. How time sweeps us through our cycles, through time, without pause."

* * *

She met John "Wolf" Larson in 1986 when he became her property manager, after answering an advertisement for the available job. They were destined to embark on a love affair. She found him handsome and he was very practical in his managing of the property. She has said it felt like *Lady Chatterley's Lover*. She is, of course, a passionate admirer of D. H. Lawrence and his writings. John, as Carolyn has written, had won first-place prizes for his art and was most accomplished with his drawings and was an excellent photographer. He also loved animals.

She wrote in an unpublished work: "I told him I liked him from the beginning, months ago, when he first came here. It was the last time I lived for a few days with my former lover. Again, the message, the synchronicity. He had come at an auspicious time, when I was barely out of the ashes of torn love. Now in this new life, he had come. He and I lived as nature, the magnificence around us, as reflections of our inner vast bounty extending forever outwards."

This is from her unpublished prose: "The best would be to lie down next to you. I just want to be a blade of grass in your meadow and breathe of your, our breeze, the environment-climate we create that is always more than anything around, the forest of you. It's the nature of you that I love. It's the you of your nature that I love. It's the garden that you are; it's the skies, yes the wilderness of you, of our exploration of ourselves together, right now apart." And: "His hands, his tree moves into me as scent, as a special musk of us. We grow together in the touch, the currenting surf of our seas, our expanding waters as they feed, nurture, move in a complimentary moisture. There's the fire of passion's unknown origin traveling our streams, lightning just above our circulations, like telephone lines, only so complex and so light and so inter-linked. There thrives again, in our ever expanding connectedness, the wells of our beings, wells as voids, wells of origin, wells of natural intimacy and our spirits ever glorified."

Carolyn and John Larson at the Ventana, Big Sur
©1990 Carolyn Mary Kleefeld Collection

Time and again in her unpublished prose, Carolyn paints with words the physical aspect of her and John's love, "Our intimacy is so powerful; it feels as if it is the archetypal force that drives the world. It is primordial and regenerating at the most rudimentary level. I am ever in gratitude for this ultimate blessing of our sacred union.

One of the unique wonders of our passion is that we both love to freefall into the moment, into an adventure of not knowing, not planning, but instead, being instruments of the universal. With our minds liberated the moment opens into an infinity of possibility and wonder. Devoted to this greater urge, we live as eternal creatures, intertwined, in continual change and motion, in a wildly exotic spell and communion.

Tonight, as you murmured in erotic tones, I was lit with the flame of you, ravished by desire. And as the night wore on, the smoldering coals of this desire fed me like a neophyte in the dawn of passion—fresh and waiting—to love you again and again as we continually create new and enriching adventures."

Carolyn wrote many poems about their relationship, including this unpublished one:

The Last Four Days

You, my love,
are the face of all lovers.
You, my love,
are love, its musk.
I have known you
before the concept of time.
I have been part of you
in some unknown way, always,
and you, of me.

You are the love of me expressed
I am you expressed
Together we branch out
touching more stars;
our roots converse.

We are of nature.
We are of the wind.

Together we bathe in the timeless beams
of the soaring winter-flower,
the phantom planet swathing us
in the life of silver,
changing us together.

We stand as two trees
in the shimmering waters.

We breathe as one with the currents,
living in the eye of the storm,
forever different.

The lightning travels through us —
the thunder, the rains, the sudden stillness.

We hear as one ear,
no longer a separation from.

We are together and a part of all,
one breath undivided.

Of the deepest root we grow,
our branches in ever expansion
and gentle touch.

Carolyn and John became friends with Jane Fonda, whom she met on horseback in her childhood, and her then husband Ted Turner, media proprietor, when Jane and Ted spent time at Ted's Big Sur residence, next door to Carolyn's house. They would head for Carolyn's BB Nest home on the opposite mountain, where John would cook dinner for everyone.

John Larson left for Alaska in 2000 when David Wayne Dunn came to live at Carolyn's "Rainbow Room", a cabin below her home, as a poet-in-residence.

After their separation in 2000, Carolyn and John's love evolved into a cherished and beloved friendship when he returned to Pankosmion in 2007 to be her "Noah of the Ark," as she described in one of her short stories, "For instance, today the older male, Noah, had driven off to shop for the creatures that lived there. He was the guardian of the extravagant gardens and woodland above the sea. He was the patriarch, grounded in the very boulders that he'd planted along the driveway some twenty years ago. He had an atavistic and quiet elegance about him. Tall, with strong broad shoulders, he was quite silent, void as a blank canvas, yet thoroughly kind and considerate to her, the creatures, and gardens. Salt of the earth, [Edmund] had called him. With black eyes that shifted like an animal's, he gazed out into the wilderness as if to constantly guard their territory. For a tall man, his tactile hands were rather small and graceful. His nose was slightly curved and short, giving his black-bearded face a handsome countenance. A saint-like man, he was a godsend, humble, devoted, and ever responsive to the pulse of every creature dwelling there. [She] could count on his loving and embodied being, regardless of the climes that invaded their Garden of Eden.

Noah: The Guardian by Carolyn Mary Kleefeld
© 2007 Carolyn Mary Kleefeld 20" x 20" Oil on Canvas

Noah's desire to assist others, particularly Carolyn, reflected his selfless nature. Being needed seemed to fan his flame, keeping him branded in his own blood."

He called Carolyn 'Little Creature' and he was 'Big Creature'. For Carolyn, John was a gentle, strong, capable, and handsome man in every respect.

Carolyn's father began to need her assistance and called for her help. As she has written, "I could not say no, but I had to leave John's and my precious love to assist Pops. John did not like the city and so our love had to change its form".

Until his sudden and unexpected death on 18th March 2018, aged 72 years-old, John was the solid foundation of their day-to-day living on the isolated mountain. Carolyn lived with John for twenty-three years and, she says: "He was kin of my soul". Carolyn was ever reliant on his commonsense and practical approach to running her property, coping with any property damage inflicted by the ferocious winters, and his driving her to places, such as Carmel, Monterey, and Los Angeles when her father, 'Pops', was alive. John, though, was far more than a property manager and beloved friend to Carolyn. He was a close confidante and someone who offered her advice when she needed a second opinion on something. I think it is true to say that John will never be replaced because of Carolyn's deep love for him. She says he was the anchor of her restless heart.

An artist of many media, John focused on animals and nature when he created, rather than humans. His love of nature and animals was apparent to all who came into contact with him; and his personal cabin, in front of Carolyn's home, was throughout the years a place where his pets, such as Needja, the adopted cat, would be cared for by this quiet, gentle, sensitive, devoted beyond measure and solitary man.

John is survived by his three sisters—Jennifer Larson, Susan Larson, and Monetha Larson Godbe—and their children.

Carolyn, John Larson, her late brother Barry, and Louise Taper
© Carolyn Mary Kleefeld Collection

This unpublished poem expresses so much in its tight eight lines, the bond between them and Carolyn's loving affection and admiration for him:

For Woof
(for John Larson)

You walk up the steps
to my redwood home
wearing your dark green sweater
that matches the leaves
of the wisteria
surrounding you
as if you were
a walking tree of a man.

As does this recent poem:

The Tallest Tree In The Forest
(for John Larson)

What would I do
without my Noah
who gives his heart
to my home, to me—
who holds the mast
of my ship steady
as the sea churns.

Such a patient man is he,
this man called Noah,
humbly caring for
all the living creatures and plants.

Without him, my ship would
tumble on a chaotic sea,
my life be turned inside out,
but Noah is here.

What a great blessing
this kind, strong man is.
Years ago I prayed
that he would come,
and how truly fortunate
I am that he did.

He must live beyond me—
I need and love him so,
need to know he is here,
need to know he is my dearest friend,
this quiet and kind man of the mountain
who lends his magnificent support,
my gentle and strong Noah,
the tallest tree in the forest.

June 19, 2015

Carolyn began a painting, *Ebony Heavens*, before John became ill. The star in the painting first appeared just before John's illness progressed, and it became increasingly prominent, becoming the strength and focus of the painting, as his illness advanced and before she, his family, and her AMA 'Carolynagens', as she calls them, knew that he would be transitioning beyond this existence. Thus, as Carolyn has said, the painting is in tribute to the rising star of John Larson, her beloved Wolf or Woofs as she nicknamed him. When he was dying, John said to Carolyn, "I'm sorry to do this to you, Little Creature."

Ebony Heavens by Carolyn Mary Kleefeld
© 2018 Carolyn Mary Kleefeld 24" x 36" Mixed media on Hard Board

* * *

David Wayne Dunn, American poet and artist, as stated in the chapter on Atoms Mirror Atoms, took up Carolyn's offer to come to Big Sur in 1998 to be a poet-in-residence in her cabin, "The Rainbow Room". David was born in Fresno, California, where he lived before residing in Big Sur. He started writing poetry as a teenager while reading Robinson Jeffers and D. H. Lawrence. About a year after his arrival, Carolyn and David, having a passion for poetry and art in common, became each other's muses and continued to develop their relationship, which blossomed into them becoming lovers.

A Bouquet Of Feelings

Joy, sadness, longing and laughter.
My lover brought
his bouquet of feelings to me —
the mistress of his dreams.

In the deep tunnel of darkness,
joy, sadness, laughter,
and longing reverberated.
And I held these feelings close
as if they were spring flowers.

Later, wrapped in the moon's arms,
we rested, rocking in a silvery light.

Then, in one flowering flame of passion,
we let go and fell into the shining seas
where we bathed, emerging as one.

They gave many poetry readings together, often turning up last-minute at open-mic event venues in places such as Monterey and San Francisco. David likes to play instruments, including the guitar and harmonica, at poetry readings and he has often provided a musical accompaniment to Carolyn's readings of her poetry. He is a prolific producer of poems, writings, paintings, drawings, outstanding photographs, and also a composer of music. His latest book is *Phantoms of Desire/Poems and Art*.

Carolyn wrote in one journal entry: "The energy of DD's psyche brings so much invention; no wonder he has been my muse for so long. No one compares to his continual improvisations, his ironic wit, and profound insights. I have some of my best laughs with him because his humor is over the top, my kind of outrageous absurdity and expansive dimension. Sometimes we tease and josh for hours."

She says of David in one unpublished poem, 'Soul Twin':

Our love is red and black,
brimming with tantric fragrance.

Yes, soul twin, I need you
with me on this journey
reflecting the miraculous mystery.

And this in one journal entry: "I only care about being with DD. Nothing else seems to really matter. He is my obsession. His energy picks me up and I become truly alive."

During the time David lived in Big Sur, they co-authored *Kissing Darkness: Love Poems and Art,* which celebrates the love and relationship between Carolyn and David via poems and artwork created by each of them. In a blurb at the back of the book, Laura Huxley declares, "Revealing the divine Eros, the untamable power of love. *Kissing Darkness* is a perfect gift for all romantics . . . of all ages." Written between 1998 and 2002, the poems in the book record David and Carolyn's passionate love.

The reader experiences the springs and the winters of their relationship. Both poets express the essence of their special love and their emotions in a direct and arresting language that draws on the Big Sur landscape and the beauty and the brutality of the natural life-forces. Thus the relationship between the two poets/artists is amplified in the symbolic intensity of their cut-off world. This is from the poem 'The Wind Moans for the Lovers' Love':

The slashing tongue
of the wind-beast howls,
admidst the snow-capped mountain peaks
angrily he demands to play,
dashing, thrashing sheets of rain
across the windowpane.

The lovers, hidden in each other's flesh
ignore the wild, wet beast outside.

Carolyn and David Wayne Dunn at Julian Pfeiffer Burns State Park
© Carolyn Mary Kleefeld Collection

Carolyn and David Wayne Dunn at Big Sur River
© Carolyn Mary Kleefeld Collection

In 2011 David moved to Carmel, but they remain very close friends and continue to inspire each other's art and writing.

Song To David

Bless you for pollinating
my poetic seed to flower.

As you breathe from the beyond,
your fountain pulses of the Beloved.

Blessings to you for being
one of God's greatest extravagances,
for bearing the injury of your splendors.

Bless you for moving the earth of me
with your deepest root,

for holding tenderly my petals within,
amidst even the most ravaging wind,
for being the wild lily
in the eternal meadows of my heart.

March 19, 1998

Your Unfurling Flame

(for DWD)

After we feast
on our own magic,
you vanish, taking
my cherished worlds with you.

Wrestling with longing,
I disappear with desire for you.

I gaze around
at the fleeting day
and notice, as if for the first time,
the trees praying in the wind.

I peer inside to see
if the tower still stands.
It has a sense of poverty now —
like a ghetto.

When you depart,
so does the Ferris wheel
of my illusions.

As you drive away,
I watch your flame unfurl —
the unwritten poem
of our passion.

As David wrote tenderly in his poem 'This Life', included in their collaborative book, *Kissing Darkness*: "Tell them even our sorrows / were magical and every pain / somehow a blessing."

And as Carolyn wrote in these two stanzas from *I Never Left You*, an unpublished poem:

Did I ever stop loving you?
Or was it always love,
even when it was war?

Our kind of love is eternal,
not just for a limited time;
it can actually increase—
even when we are apart.

Carolyn continues to see David, mostly on her visits to his home in Carmel, and she is always astonished by his devotion to his work and what he produces as a poet, artist, and photographer: "We roamed about while his car was being repaired. We went to the most enchanting Mexican coffee shop and had German chocolate cake and hot chocolate with coffee. Quite delicious. I haven't had bakery for a while. DD rambled on with very intriguing communing. Eventually, we picked up the car, and went. Then to the Magic Castle of DD's. What an amazing amount of creative energy. So much artwork. Some I loved. All of such fertile essence. I played some piano again with DD. So magical. It's astonishing the way he set up his keyboard. He has so many talents. I love the drawings, poetry, music, photography. He is a never ceasing pulsing engine of creation."

She has said about David, as recently as 2016 in a journal entry, "He is a blessed gift in my life, an extravagant soul."

* * *

In 2002, Carolyn met David Campagna, an American film and television actor and artist (who would later become her husband) when Linda Jacobson, teacher and an artist friend of Carolyn's, brought her students to Carolyn's home, which Linda did once a year as part of her art course. David was one of Linda's students on that visit to the Big Sur mountaintop. He was born in 1946 in San Jose, California. His great grandfather on his mother's side was Portuguese and emigrated to America in 1849 or 1850, according to David in an interview with American writer and sculptor John Dotson, which was a Special Supplement to *The Seventh Quarry Swansea Poetry Magazine* in 2016. His father's side originated from Italy.

David Campagna, Carolyn's fourth husband
© Carolyn Mary Kleefeld Collection

David grew up in Fremont, a city in California's San Francisco Bay Area. David recalled in the interview: "Fremont was a car culture. I was always ready to get outta there. San Francisco was changing. Little did I know it was becoming the center of the universe. Fremont is within an hour of the ocean, and I surfed too. I was a part of that culture. I would go over to Santa Cruz. The only thing with the surfing bit was that I wasn't that good! That can get dangerous. I had a couple of very near death experiences. The other thing was I loved football, captain of the football team."

He also spoke of his initial interest in art and his beginnings as an artist, "I took art in high school and did some painting. Everybody really liked it. I've always loved painting ever since I first saw Jackson Pollock and the new modern painters. I saw a couple of Richard Diebenkorn paintings in L.A.—the *Ocean Park* paintings. I didn't know who he was. I was very impressed. I love Mark Rothko. And one other would be Diego Rivera. I've always admired Diego Rivera. But when I first started really painting, taking it seriously, realizing I was leading the artist's life anyway, was about 1991."

In response to John Dotson's question about how he became interested in acting, he replied:

"You know, a typical unhappy childhood. I would sit there and watch television whenever and get carried away, and I thought, this is what I would like to do. I realized later on I was escaping into that world. But as a child I remember looking and seeing Perry Mason, with Raymond Burr, and pointing at the television and saying, Oh, that's what I want to do! What I want to do is be Perry Mason! My mother took it that I wanted to be an attorney. So for the rest of my childhood, my mother said, "David's gonna be a lawyer. David wants to be a lawyer." It was hard to tell her, No, I want to *play* a lawyer on television."[1]

David took acting and the History of Theater at Foothill College in Los Altos Hills, California, where he learned a lot in a year, before quitting. He recalled that it had a very good drama department and a very knowledgeable head of the department, Doyne Mraz, who was the professor. In 1972, David headed for Los Angeles where he established himself as an actor. He based himself in 1973 in a West Hollywood apartment, where he remained for almost forty-four years.

He was hired as a page for ABC Television, working on several network shows, including *The Merv Griffin Show, Laverne and Shirley, Happy Days, The Odd Couple,* and *The Lawrence Welk Show.* Under the tutelage of acting teacher Jeff Corey, he became a soap opera actor, with roles In *General Hospital* and *The Young and the Restless.*

David became Hollywood actor Christopher Walken's stand-in and stunt double in more than 15 films over 20 years. David told the *East Bay Times* in an interview in 2006, "Usually, Chris will come in and do the scene once, and I'll observe it very closely. I have to watch every detail—where he's sitting, how he holds a cigarette. If you miss a move even for a few seconds, it can be critical. Then they use me sometimes, instead of Chris."[2]

Carolyn says people found David most charismatic, charming and handsome; and he became a shining star, all to make Carolyn happy. The Beverly Hills Hotel, located on Sunset Boulevard in Beverly Hills, California, would become their base when Carolyn spent time with David in Los Angeles. One of the world's best known hotels, it is closely associated with Hollywood film stars, rock stars, and celebrities. Past guests include Katharine Hepburn, Marilyn Monroe, John Lennon, Richard Burton and Elizabeth Taylor.

Even at the start of their relationship, her journal entries capture the wonderful times they had together: "I had a totally pleasurable day with DC. We met at 1:00. He has a new white jeep, like a toy milk truck. We went to the museum, saw the Pompeii exhibit—incredulous how marble lasts for thousands of years, sometimes untarnished. It's hard to relate with my own works except through the beauty, craftsmanship and the history of that time. And that's enough!

"Then we went up to DC's place, which looked empty but cluttered. Then to the hotel at my suggestion. It was great. We ordered food, snacks, and then had a bath. Then loved each other. It felt so good to be in his arms. Also, the movie *Little Ashes* was most intriguing, most aesthetic, with incredible faces and clothes and setting. Tragic love story between Lorca and Salvador Dalí who was cast as a young very narcissistic mad genius. Lorca was romantic, sensitive and tragic, being assassinated as a young man about thirty years old. I so enjoyed the sensuous and erotic history of Lorca and Dalí. Then we had a better than good time–great and erotic. We were together for ten hours and it flew by, like birds made white in the sun's radiance.

"Then I called DC at 6 and he came over at 7:30 bringing a bouquet of roses and maiden fern. It felt romantic and fun to have our date. We went to Chin-Chin on Sunset for Chinese food—enjoyed the people-watching and of course DC, then to Book Soup. Then walked a few blocks up and down.

"Then went back to the BH Hotel, had a nice bath, and an especially satisfying time together. He felt most nourishing and erotic and I told him. He stayed until 1:30. Then I packed (had a lot of energy).

And: "[I] met DC. We went to the Jasmine Gardens. [It was] quite magical and splendorous. DC kissed me a few times and I was transported beyond simply the jungle gardens, [beyond the] orange koi and dragonflies. His kiss is the kiss I've waited a lifetime for. Words are not able to express the magnitude of what I feel in his kiss.

"We had a great time driving home the rest of the day. He is such a great navigator. He found [my former] house on Haynes, [and the homes of my neighbors,] the Melvin's and the Chinese people—none [is] recognizable, like a person's face after so many years. My past lives were revisited. We went up Crescent Heights and I think I saw that house with the West Hollywood view. We listened to my CD around there and kissed again a few times. He seemed moved by my voice on my latest reading. Then, around 6, we went to Chin Chin. So enjoyed the sun on my back and looking at DC's handsomeness, like a Roman god, bronze-skinned and blue-eyed, the people going by. Then back to the hotel [for] a glorious bubble bath and lots of kisses before and after. Leonard Cohen was with us, as usual.

"The words that come to me about DC and the evening are: erotic, sensuous, hot, fun, yummy, blue eyes, handsome, sexy, passionate, comfortable, and what more is there? Oh yes, satisfied and fulfilled. I'm so happy we have plans every day through Saturday. That way, we get to enjoy each other more and more without a fast departure. What a truly wonderful lover he is—of the heart, of the body, of the soul. He likes to wander and live in a Zen-like fashion. He is very together and caring."

This is another entry, three years later: "I'm so crazy about DC that nothing else can hold a torch. Of course, I still love so very much the other angels in my life, but he is my torch of passion, the light for my heart and soul. He is the muse of majestic passion.

"What a sense of vulnerability there is in such love. I feel reborn in the moment just thinking of him, of beloved David. I'm crazy about so many things about him—his easy going Mediterranean temperament, his sense of humor, his eroticism, sexuality, his capabilities, his philosophy, (the)abundance of loving he shows me in every way—[his] thoughtfulness, care, consideration, devotedness. How can I count all his ways? His strength of mind and body—and I'm sure there is more. The way he is with people. . ."

The Bikers, Carolyn and David © Carolyn Mary Kleefeld Collection

Carolyn told David Jay Brown in her latest interview with him, "For many years now, my sweetheart David Campagna has been my primary muse. David is an extraordinary man, actor, and artist brimming with love lyrics and brilliant wit, who has created his own striking abstracts. Our regenerative love is the catalyst for our lives.

"David has inspired many paintings and poems that have been exhibited and published here in the US and internationally. My book of love poems titled *The Divine Kiss* was written in his honor, and the paintings and poems from that book have been exhibited at The Karpeles Manuscript Library Museum in Santa Barbara, CA, and Shreveport, LA. After traveling across the world to see Leonard Cohen, DC got to know him for a short time. And when he met Leonard Cohen at Cedars Sinai Medical Center, he dragged himself, attached to a chemo machine, over to Leonard to give him a copy of *The Divine Kiss* Leonard said, 'I am sure you know this was written in your honor'. *The Divine Kiss* has also been translated into Japanese, Italian, Sicilian, Greek, and Persian.

Carolyn and David © Carolyn Mary Kleefeld Collection

"As you know, when romantic passion and creative expression merge, it is both exhilarating and ultimately fulfilling. Passion has always propelled my life and artwork. Of course, love has a myriad of other shades besides the romantic, which can also enrich and expand my life and palette.

"Just to give you an example of how emotions give birth to my art, recently, as I was working on *The Eternal Quest,* a painting from my 'Lovers' series, I felt a surge of passion move through me and directly embody the work. This was truly thrilling to experience. I became the receptive instrument, observing my own experiment, while 'passion' itself painted my partner's handsome and courageous face.

"As TAOists, favorite way of living for David C and me is we love to freefall into the moment, into the adventure of not knowing, not planning, but instead, being instruments of spontaneity and synchronicity. With our minds liberated, the present moment opens into an infinity of possibility and wonder. This 'beloved dance' can only thrive from the eternal, which has no mind, but simply beholds and embraces the pure and golden heart born anew in the moment.

"The dance of love, which brings me fully into the unfolding moment.

"My beloved David has been dealing with some intense health challenges these past few years, so we have been on a rocky journey together. Yet, I have learned and experienced so much because of our magnetic and romantic love. Living on the abyss has brought us even further vulnerability and intimacy. And the grist from this shared challenge has poured into an ever-expanding oeuvre of artwork that records these climes of romantic and eternal love, healing, and transformation.

"So, I continue to experiment."[3]

Carolyn and David travelled the world together until just before he transitioned, to such places as Hawaii, London, Wales, Paris, Venice, and Greece. It was David who made it easy for Carolyn to take up travelling again from her Big Sur bird's nest of a home.

The world travellers © Carolyn Mary Kleefeld Collection

This is Carolyn's recollection of her visit to Crete, Greece's largest Island, a pilgrimage to the world of one of her all-time favourite writers, Nikos Kazantzakis, where they visited his grave, located at the highest point of the Venetian Walls of Heraklion, the Martinengo Bastion: "Here in Crete we visit what was Nikos Kazantzakis' father's home, which is now a museum. Unfortunately, they ruined the essence of what the house was really like in the slick mask, the exterior. We didn't go inside because it was too late in the day, but the old street next to it was enchanted, and a little peasant woman all hunchbacked was sweeping away. She looked straight into me as I was feeling that she was a reincarnation of NK's passion for the old wise peasant people he encountered. A few other old women dressed in black looked at us—I, dressed in my colors, and seemed in their contemptuous eyes to condemn and resent my freedom, probably their religion being their imprisonment.

"I wept silently while sitting on NK's cement grave. His words 'I fear nothing. I have no hope. I am free,' are messages to my soul. DC and I took photos of each other as we stood up against his tall cross. The cement area of his grave was quite large, and nearby was the smaller grave of Eleni. I felt NK's essence within me and also Eleni's. As I felt them in my blood consciousness, the wind carried some mysterious sounds as if in response to my feelings. It was uncanny how DC found the place. He is a brilliant navigator and adventurer. I feel most fortunate that I know and love him so."

The Spirit Of Crete

(for DC)

A sliver of moon
haunts the Cretan sea
as we stroll, arm and arm,
down a dark, dirt path
to an ocean-side restaurant.

Here, a Grecian feast
refreshes our souls
and the lunar spell
with its silvery beams
dapples the lapping waters,
the tidal rhythms in cadence
with our flow of intimacy.

Nearby, a hungry cat
hunts for treats,
her beseeching eyes
glimmering in the darkness.

Enlivened by
the feral elements that be,
the spirit of Crete
pulses through our veins.

And our hearts wander
the soulful lyrics
of this Cretan night.

After visiting Nikos & Eleni Kazantzakis' grave in Heraklion, Crete

September 13, 2012

These are some snippets from entries about a visit to Paris with David, residing in the Shangri-La Hotel on Avenue d'Iéna, and where they saw Leonard Cohen in concert: "The Louvre was so crowded and huge that between the swarms of people, [oh] the enormity of the Louvre, I couldn't wait to escape. It was hot and stuffy in those windowless rooms. [There were] lines of people to see *The Mona Lisa*, which I grew up with a copy of in our Santa Monica living room as a child. I always felt she was seeing me no matter where I was. My mother had that kind of beauty as a young woman–a kind of other worldly beauty, ethereal.

"We did have a miraculous day—went to the cemetery and saw Jim Morrison's grave and Chapel. Mostly it was deeply touching to experience the character and antiquity of all the little mausoleums or sepulchers, the moss growing and the cracking cement. It was like a village of the dead, their fame bringing endless tourists.

"Today, visiting Montmartre was the same—throngs of people like Coney Island, everyone drawn to where the famous painters, artists lived so long ago. It's impossible not to feel the great loss of a place that now is so corrupted. DC and I have the artist within us. We don't need to try to find what now is lost. It only makes us covet what creative energy we do have.

"Then we went to the Eiffel Tower, which again, had a mile-long line. The great triumphs of all the monuments, churches, and incredible accomplishments now bring all these tourists. Since David knows the history of all this, it is more interesting than just being a sightseer.

It was an experience of a lifetime to be with Leonard and his band of masters, with Leonard speaking French and singing one song in French. His indomitable vitality, passion, and spell-binding magic permeated us beyond yet deep in our core."

Carolyn and David in Paris
© 2012 Carolyn Mary Kleefeld Collection

The day of David's diagnosis of a terminal illness, in 2014, he spontaneously brought Carolyn to a menagerie in downtown Los Angeles where all different kinds of butterflies were living and flying about. Later, when he was close to passing on, David asked Carolyn to be the butterfly for both of them when he shed his earthly cocoon. He said he would be inside Carolyn forever. Carolyn has said she later had a dream that like a Lazarus he came from above and became part of her. He was by her side for a second before he departed. She told him how much she loved him and he vanished.

By 2016, David was suffering from the chemo and radiation, yet they came together so that they could go to Venice in Italy for her birthday. Carolyn, wanting to fulfill his wish, despite her concerns that such a trip would be too arduous for his failing body, accompanied him in May of that year. She wrote at the time: "The beauty of this decaying city is truly awesome. The primal green waters of the canals, the black gondolas, the gondoliers in dark blue and white stripes having traffic jams because of the over-exploding tourism, [and] the enchantment of these ancient fairy castles set upon sand pilings makes what DC and I are experiencing almost match in the surrealism. DC looked like a Roman god when he sat up in this bed of ours today with his noble Roman profile and all he is, filling my heart with infinite passion and compassion. I pray I can keep my health through this, so I can be there, here for and with him.

I like the Italian nature as I experience them—strong, lusty, passionate, outgoing, hospitable.

Late today, after having our snack near St Marks's at the fabulously charming café, the Florian Restaurant (300 years old), we took a ride home on a black gondola, moving deftly through the narrow canals passing the old crumbling Venetian houses in which only the higher part of the house could be used. All the bridges add to the romanticism, the beguiling auras of Venetzia. We also went to the Jewish Ghetto, which looked more authentic without the many brand names stores hawking their wares.

"Today's so-called 'civilization' with all their selfies and cell phones trying to capture this Renaissance Museum also is surreal to see, to view what happens through time–not only to ourselves, our bodies, faces, brains, and hearts, but to the human mode of the day. From art, architecture, creation to this convoluted madness of cell phone implosions and selfies, which seem to be desperately attempting to get something by copying it on camera. How many who use all these mechanical means, how many are experiencing anything in an artistic-feeling way? The faces seem robotized and [on] a kind of trance state of a kind of oblivion."

Earlier in their beloved relationship, Carolyn's deep love for David made her consider the idea of buying a property in Los Angeles, where she and David could set up home. The thought of such a place weaves its way through many of her journal entries. She and David even looked at some properties, but the frantic and very materialistic way of life in Los Angeles, which Carolyn could only deal with in small doses always became the deciding factor in them not buying a property there. "Do I want a love-nest with DC there? Or wouldn't it work, meaning more responsibility, and the hotel (the Beverly Hills Hotel) offers far more freedoms for both of us. I don't really need to move there. It could be disorienting to be in that chaos and value systems I left behind over thirty years ago. I need to be able to put my roots back in the soil while I'm in Big Sur, gather the essence of my selves together into one enrichment of integration."

Carolyn says that David's radiant smile made everything possible. She wrote in her Introduction to the Special Supplement to *The Seventh Quarry Swansea Poetry Magazine*, about David, "An ordinary person, supposedly, he is an extraordinary man. His way of living is an art in itself. *Living* is his art.

"Wherever he goes people start laughing and remembering the happy part of life because of his hilarious sense of humor. The medical staff welcome his incredible spirit and humor. When he grew up he created this humor, not consciously, but he created it in childhood, always finding a way to make sad people laugh, to create a happier environment for other people. He brings that to them. It's a magical place that breaks through to joy. He brings more joy to the world. Everyone loves him.

"David took care of his mother for the last few years of her life. During that time, he gave up his work in Hollywood, turning down offers so that he could be at her side in her last years. She had been a supreme challenge, and he was able to turn this around and give her everything she never had. He hardly ever left her side. She could not bear it even when he tried to leave her side for five minutes. He gave her so much joy and adventure in her last years. Carolyn told David he was a saint and he replied, 'the neighborhood saint perhaps.'

"David is a total hero to me, a Don Quixote in his times. He is living through an enduring uphill battle with cancer, and he is definitely doing this in the most brave and magnificent way—beyond any Oscar-winning roles. His life movie that he is starring in now is his greatest role. Only the rare few can live out such a life with this much courage, humor, love, and valiance. I'm just blown away by the noble character of this man dealing with chronic pain with determination, strength, and humor. Through all these years of endurance, he has been and continues to be loving and magnificent always. This, to me, is his life beyond life, beyond any possible role."[4]

There was a prodigious outpouring of poems, other writings, and artwork from

Carolyn during David's illness. This is from a prose-piece entitled 'A Don Quixote of Our Times (for DC)':

"Tomorrow morning, he will take another test to determine the status of his health, yet another stress for his silken, apricot body. And here I am obsessing, helpless to do more than love him. The difficulty is feeling his suffering, although he is an expert at disguising it.

"For now, hell still has us in its fangs. There's nothing we can do but hang in there and hope for the best as we try to make possible our impossible dream. It sounds simple, but is a continual challenge. We have to keep reminding ourselves to just be in the moment–as we realize the *moment* is all we have. As Leonard Cohen said to David, 'They just keep us hanging on.' David made the impossible possible. He transcended the physical trauma somehow, and his spirit ascended all the tortures. We always had our magic."

This beautiful poem and beautiful prose-piece are representative of so many:

Reborn In The Instant
(for DC)

I have waited in
my sacred temple
for your emergence
from a death haunt.

And now, I sense my chambers
emptied of your birth,
and watch as the sun of you
takes a new form.

Now we have a chance
to breathe deeply again
of the emerald whispers,
to be reborn in the instant

to ascend into a radiant new life—
an ever deeper embrace.

Carolyn needed to write. As she records in a journal entry, written after she had read some of her poems to David in their suite at the Beverly Hills Hotel, "The need for me to create the work is coming from my own desire to heal. So the organic process of it, the creating, the editing, and after[wards the] re-experiencing [of] it, is an organic thing [which] is capable of giving me back what it is—like a living process that can be metabolized. It certainly gave me a direct hit as to its importance as a great healing art that is as never before. Since my work comes from the need to expand in my consciousness, to read it and share it becomes truly a healing art—both for me in all aspects of it and in the sharing."

These writings became the manuscript that would become Carolyn's book, *Immortal Seeds: Bearing Gold from the Abyss*, a collection of poetry, prose, and art, which Carolyn created during David's illness and in the year or so after his transition. The following piece of prose is from *Immortal Seeds*.

The Skin Of Faith
(for DC)

Wearing only the skin of my faith, I quietly enter your dark bedroom, where you are sleeping deeply. Kneeling by your bed, I cover you with an ambrosia of love, with blessings from the divine miracles, with fortitude to cross the abyss. You don't know I am here, but perhaps my prayers will make a difference, as I feel them so strongly on a molecular level.

Yes, wearing only the skin of faith, I infuse you, my beloved angel, with divine blessings and call forth the strength that you are, to cross the abyss. Amen.

She and David married on Valentine's Day 2017, in suite #425 in The Beverly Hills Hotel, Los Angeles. In his expressions of love for Carolyn, some of his nicknames for her were Baby Cakes, Glass Angel, Wild Cupcake, Magnificent She-Creature, Dream Angel, She-Devil, and Amber Bear. When he was close to passing on, he nicknamed her Half a Snowflake, probably because he thought she looked so forlorn.

The hands of Carolyn and David on their wedding day in the Beverly Hills Hotel, Los Angeles © 2017 Carolyn Mary Kleefeld Collection

When going through the most difficult times during David's illness, he showed Carolyn what infinite love is through his love for her. Because of his love for her, Carolyn said she was guided into the sacred chambers of infinite love. She recounted he "whistled in the face of death."

David died *three weeks later*, on 6th March 2017, of esophageal cancer, which was diagnosed three years earlier. His obituary appeared in the Los Angeles Times on 25th March and 26th, 2017. It included this: "He died as he lived his life, with style and grace, breathing his last breath in a suite at the Beverly Hills Hotel with his beloved Carolyn at his side. David was an actor, an artist, and a world traveler but he was much more than the disciplines he chose to pursue. His thirst for knowledge was unquenchable, only a small evidence of which was the thousand-book personal library he left. David was fascinated by Eastern religion and traveled to places like Kathmandu, trekking the mountains of Nepal to further his search. He went with Larry and Fran Levy and their daughter to China and Japan. But no matter how serious his quest for inner peace, he maintained a sharp sense of humor with a rapier wit, always ready with a quick barb to deflate someone's misplaced ego."

And: "David had several love affairs in his life, but by far he saved his greatest for last. He and Carolyn were true soulmates who fully adored each other, and sanctified this love in their marriage this past Valentine's Day. It gave all of his friends great pleasure to see that he had found such a wonderful woman who understood what a great guy he was. His last thoughts were not about his fate but rather that of Carolyn as he asked his friends to make sure she was okay. David was cremated with his ashes sent to Carolyn. He is survived by Carolyn and the many friends who adored him."

Carolyn feels she has a kind of calling with regard to helping family, lovers and indeed beloved friends (like her father, her mother, John Larson, Laura Huxley and Edmund Kara) into their transitions to the beyond.

David continues to inspire Carolyn, which is seen in the poems, writings, and the paintings she continues to create about him. This is also from Carolyn's book "Immortal Seeds: Bearing Gold from the Abyss".

Your Invisible Embrace
(for DC)

O my angel now in transit,
your flame still possesses me,
as I stumble into an unknown dawn.

I see you in everything,
my ennobled heart of love.
You ever guide me through
the darkness of an uncharted path.

Although your flesh has departed,
your spirit still enraptures me.
The ocean below echoes of
its tidal longing.
And the haunt of a growing darkness
sleeps with me.

I await your invisible embrace
as the morning seeks dawn.

The silence of my home
is clothed in grief,
but the little birds of morning
still will sing.

The blind forces have been fed
by a sacrifice eternal.
Perhaps they are assuaged for now.

Come to me now,
my beloved husband,
illuminate the darkness
with your ever-brilliant light.

It is fitting, though, to finish this chapter on love as an inspiration with a poem from *The Divine Kiss*, the book of poems and paintings inspired by David Campagna and a celebration of Carolyn's and David's remarkable love for each other.

The Kiss

(for DC)

Tonight, the kiss I've dreamed of,
the kiss of a lifetime, is here.

And now we hug and kiss
and kiss and love–
exploding the moment,

as if we were an extravagant bouquet
of burgeoning buds and stamens.

Like creatures dashing through the forest,
we tumble into each other's arms,
our mouths and leafy boughs entwined.

Some strange and wondrous magnet
is drawing us together
like orbiting stars, carrying us
beyond the dust of ourselves.

Divine Kiss by Carolyn Mary Kleefeld
© 2012 Carolyn Mary Kleefeld
20" x 20" Oil on Canvas

147

Chapter 9

LAURA HUXLEY, WIFE OF ALDOUS HUXLEY

✧

"Our beloved one, always my torch of love and inspiration."
—Carolyn Mary Kleefeld

The first meeting between Carolyn and Laura Huxley occurred in the late 1980s, at a meeting in Hollywood of the Albert Hofmann Foundation, where Carolyn served on the board. Dr. Albert Hofmann, who was born in Switzerland in 1906, is famous for being the inventor/"father" of LSD, lysergic acid diethalymide. He was the first to synthesise, ingest, and learn of the psychedelic effects of the drug. The exploratory work by this then unknown chemist at his Sandoz Laboratory in Basle, Switzerland, "turned on" the generation of the 1960s. In late life he called LSD "medicine for the soul" but was actually critical of its misuse by that counter-culture of the 1960s. Carolyn met Albert Hofmann at Oscar Janiger's home.

The non-profit Foundation was founded in 1988, and its mission statement reads, "Throughout history people have used mind-expanding substances to explore consciousness and enhance their lives. Our purpose at the Albert Hofmann Foundation is to gather the records of these endeavours and to further the understanding and responsible application of psychedelic substances in the investigation of both individual and collective consciousness."

Carolyn and Laura remained close friends until Laura's death, when she was ninety-six years, on 13th December 2007. Like Carolyn's friendship with Edmund Kara, Laura and Carolyn added so much to each other's lives.

Carolyn with Laura Archera Huxley, wife of Aldous Huxley
© Carolyn Mary Kleefeld Collection

Born in Italy in 1911, Laura Archera Huxley was a highly intelligent and very talented woman. She made her mark as a musician, studying the violin, and in 1937, aged twenty-six, she performed at Carnegie Hall, her debut in America. She was an author, freelance documentary film-maker, and a lay psychotherapist. She first entered into English writer, novelist and philosopher Aldous Huxley's life (1894-1963) in 1948 when she had the idea of making a documentary film. They married in 1956. *You Are Not the Target*, her book on self-help, was written in 1963, the year that Aldous died on 22nd November. Following his death, she devoted herself to ensuring his remarkable works, such as the dystopian novel *Brave New World* and *The Doors of Perception*, a philosophical essay that details his experiments with mescaline, would be remembered. Her 1968 memoir, *This Timeless Moment: A Personal View of Aldous Huxley*, about her seven-year marriage to Aldous, published after his death, reveals intimate aspects of the character of a profound thinker and pioneering novelist of the 20th century.

These are some of Carolyn's comments on the book and on Laura and Aldous in two of her journal entries: "Somehow I found Laura's *The Timeless Moment* in my hands, and I'm reading it and wonderfully so. It's most inspirational and perhaps will lead to reading more of Aldous' work. I have the books Laura gave me. What an honor, I realize now, to be given these books by my beloved Laura and the magnificent Aldous. In this reading of them both, I am aware of a new sense of inspiration coming.

"I've been reading Laura's *Timeless* Moment and feel very fueled by her writing, life, and stories and of course, learning more about Aldous and her. How truly remarkable and so right that they met, married, and were such a union of positive forces in our times. I felt the reassuring haunt of sadness after putting the book down, after absorbing her giant pulse of being and missing her. Somehow I feel I've known Aldous's face, that he is familiar, as if from an unknown time, such handsome sensitivity and kindness flowing in his being. There is so much to learn from these two great personages, not only their knowledge, values and interests, but the very beingness of them as individuals.

"I think of my times with Laura in her sun-drenched living room, of the occasion when we sat together on the couch, holding hands, when people had come over for her birthday, and her murmuring to me, 'You are the biggest character here' and I whispering back, 'What about you?' There were so many things to remember of her, such gracious hospitality, even when she was quite unwell—how we would dance to the wonderful music, and she would move with us, and sometimes stand above on the staircase and drop scarves down for us to use with our dancing. The joyful memories are so numerous and nourishing that to grieve seems out of place with the completeness she was able to impart. I remember when I first began to visit her I had been living in such isolation that I found it difficult sometimes to be comfortable socially. As time went on, the alienation began to melt and my earlier easier sociability returned.

"One of the many outstanding facets to Laura and Aldous' relationship was their ability to be so in love and also so capable of expressing it, yet able to love others without possessiveness or jealousies. Laura actually helped Maria (Aldous' previous wife of thirty-five years) to die, which I hadn't realized. It was all about helping others and loving in such awareness, sublime grace. No wonder they were leaders of the human potential movement. They lived it as individuals in creative imagination themselves."

151

Laura was the founder of "Children: Our Ultimate Investment", a non-profit organization, in 1978. Now steered by her adopted daughter, Karen Pfeiffer, it is a foundation that has the education and parenting of young people as its main focus.

Carolyn, as stated previously, is someone who takes the synchronicity in our lives seriously, and her meeting and friendship with Laura Huxley is one that certainly seems to have been destined to happen to both women. In some ways, her friendship with Laura linked her to Aldous Huxley who was a dear friend of English novelist, poet and painter D. H. Lawrence (1885–1930), whose works remain among Carolyn's favourite all-time writings. Garsington Manor near Oxford in England, the home of English aristocrat and society hostess Lady Ottoline Morrell (1873-1938), was a gathering place for intellectual writers such as Huxley, Lawrence, and America poet T. S. Eliot. Lady Ottoline Morrell introduced Huxley to Lawrence in 1915.

Carolyn would visit Laura at her home in Los Angeles twice a month, when they would engage in passionate discussions, and Carolyn would read from her oncoming books and her poetry to Laura, who had become blind.

Laura's passing in 2007 unlocked poems and paintings in Carolyn, such was her love for her older friend and how much she was inspired by Laura. Carolyn wrote in her unpublished journal entries in 2009, "I dreamt about the youthful Laura Huxley last night (really this morning). She had dyed her white hair black, and she was wearing the plastic visor-like glasses that we both wore when she was alive. A wonderful dream to be with her again. What an individualistic and great character she was and is, living on in my heart and spirit. Then, the fact we both swam and had pools. After more reflection, I think her hair was dyed black because she was an opposite from me in many ways. Yet we shared vital predominant values and certain mutualities."

This is one of a number of poems that Carolyn wrote about Laura:

O Eternal Flower

in memory of beloved Laura Archera Huxley

O Eternal Flower,
how fragrant your scent
and how far-reaching your roots
Although you've come and gone,
you're still here, nonetheless.
Somehow, concepts of life and death
are too limited
for your present formlessness.

No, it's not real to me
that you've died.
It's no more real than
life's other illusions.

My truth is, O Eternal Flower,
that you still exist — outside of time,
a scent that forever lingers.
How infinite your spirit
as it travels the universe
and mocks the smallness
we dote upon.

O Eternal Flower,
how fragrant your scent,
how far-reaching your roots.

No, it's not real to me
that you've died —
no more real than
life's other illusions.

Carolyn also wrote in a journal entry in February 2009, "Ronna (Carolyn's friend and art consultant) and I watched the movie *Huxley on Huxley*, about Laura and Aldous, produced by Mary Ann Braubach. It was well made and Laura, most entrancing—Aldous, captivating and elegant, really inspiring people. I realize I feel so close to LH, that her fame is not what attracted me, but that who I knew her to be so inspired my life that to be part of her life was so enhancing and expanding. I can see how my life was changed without her beloved friendship, and also the life I had with those family members and friends she had introduced to me. To see the film certainly reminded me of her most fabulous being, but it also left me feeling the loss of her."

Laura Huxley was someone who recognized the original and special writer that Carolyn is, and she wrote a beautiful piece that was included in Carolyn's book *The Alchemy of Possibility*, which was published in 1998. This is part of what Laura wrote: "Like all nature mystics, Carolyn has a symbiotic relationship with nature. *The Alchemy of Possibility* might remind us, not through statistics but through poetic prose, that the Golden Rule is to be applied to every tree, every rock, every creature, and every thing on the planet. The poem *is you, is me* says it all."

In 2008, a poem Carolyn wrote to commemorate her admiration for Aldous Huxley and his influence on aspects of her thinking, entitled *Being Silence*, was read at the opening of the Fourth International Aldous Huxley Symposium at the Huntington Library in San Marino, California. She was also asked by Dr. Bernfried Nugel of the Centre for Aldous Huxley Studies in Germany and who is also Chairman of the University of Münster, whom she had met more than once at Laura Huxley's Los Angeles home, to give a talk at a conference being held at Oxford University in 2014, but she had to decline. She said this in her journal entry: "[I am still] dealing with whether or not to go to Oxford and share the intimacy that I had with Laura—poems and prose—or whether to let go of any attachment to appear there based on others being impressed with 'Oxford.' Already I don't think it fits with me. Having to be there at 9:30, across the world, for a twenty-minute presentation doesn't really fit. There are many scholars who could do a far better presentation."

After Laura's death, Carolyn continued to make visits to Los Angeles, to spend time with their mutual friends. Her journal entries over the years are dotted with the enriching times she spent with them. "Evan (her driver and dear friend) when

154

she visited LA) picked me up and took me to Paul's (Dr. Paul Fleiss, an American pediatrician and author known for his unconventional medical views). The air was cold, but the day, sunny. We all went to George and Peggy's (the DiCaprios, father and stepmother of Hollywood actor Leonardo) and then went up to Laura's and hiked around the Hollywood sign. Wonderful walk, seeing the reservoir, the dog park, and Laura's old previous home from different angles. It looks like a huge box now, no nostalgic lacy feel, no softness. At least the arches continue to be there. It was twilight, and every leaf shone in the amber light.

"We then went to Peggy and George's and saw a Fran Lebowitz documentary. What an unusual character, but intelligent. Then the five of us went to the Steve Allen Theater (on Hollywood Blvd) and saw a hilarious play—Tom Murrin, who was a riot. It was just the kind of play, different and ridiculous, that I had been thinking was needed, after reading Daniil Kharms. It's like magic that the first day I'm here, just what I needed happened—the absurd, the laughter, and the great company of Evan, George, Paul, and Peggy. I met Tom Murrin whose performance was really mesmerizing. A lot of high energy at the theater."

Sometimes Carolyn would be accompanied to Los Angeles by a beloved friend, such as Patricia of AMA, Ronna, Carolyn's artistic friend, or Val Leveroni Corral, Director at Wo/Men's Alliance for Medical Marijuana (WAMM). Whilst in Los Angeles, Carolyn would sometimes get to see her friends Linda Jacobson, a noted artist and much admired art teacher, and Jai Italiaander, who is highly regarded in the entertainment industry for her confidential and deeply accurate astrological readings.

Though even when in Los Angeles to see such dear friends, the poet in Carolyn is always alert and she pulls back the shiny bright carpet of Hollywood and reveals the dark sadness beneath it: "The congestion in LA provides no possible future—only the curdling of those superficial values, mindsets, and delusions. The women in their twenties and thirties exemplify what females from their part of the jungle are supposed to look like—with their 6-inch heels and tiny wrists with big implants, faces—or masks that all look alike. They are like dolls made from the surgery cookie cutter. When a female there is older than the prime, they better have hooked some money because they will be programmed to have surgery, and they'll need that expenditure to feel self-assured in an unreal way. Or better said, to achieve a false identity composed of looking a certain way, pleasing a man enough to be supported by them financially—truly another disguised form of sexual slave trade.

These cutouts hardly bother to look at you. Unless you have a large pocketbook appearance and you are shopping in the stores they work in, you are meaningless to them. Money, age, sex, power—that's it in the Hollywood jungle. It's totally primitive behind its plastic surgical masks."

Aldous Huxley, of course, was always aware of mankind's continuous fall from its true potential. It is a concern and a theme that appears constantly in Carolyn's journal entries and her other writings. She does see some positive light in the same journal entry: "Of course, I'm sure there are exceptions, people who hang out on the outskirts and create their other realities. And of course, everyone lives under the umbrella of illusion. No matter who we are or what systems we've inherited, we all need our dreams, illusions to make life possible, to endure and enjoy."

Also, despite the pitfalls of the gaudy and in-your-face materialism of aspects of Los Angeles, Carolyn's human relationships there make such visits worthwhile, "But one's friends do make the absolute difference. There, one can feel loved, be personalized, instead of being an emblem."

On 14th and 15th December 2013, Carolyn and David Campagna attended a memorial fundraiser for the charity, "Children: Our Ultimate Investment", set up by Laura when she was alive and steered by her adopted daughter Karen Pfeiffer after Laura's death. Various friends also attended, such as Dr. Paul Fleiss and George and Peggy DiCaprio. Carolyn read a poem, 'I Found My Soul', and a few short prose pieces about Laura.

I Found My Soul

for Laura Archera Huxley

In the grace of
a dying garden,
I found my soul.

In the crisp, golden leaves,
in the broken tile,
under the arches of a dead history,

my soul appeared, naked amid
the crumbling tower of yesterday.

In the shady nooks,
the secrets lie with blue lips
waiting to be revived
by a red generation.

I swim in the old pool
with new water and
the light of the future
beams through the boughs
of ancient oak.

Old and new fuse
in my bloodstreams,
in the primal waters.

2007

(Inspired by my swim at the Huxley home in the Hollywood Hills, California)

Carolyn's personal photo of Laura and Aldous Huxley
© Carolyn Mary Kleefeld Collection

Carolyn's personal photo of Aldous Huxley
© Carolyn Mary Kleefeld Collection

Chapter 10

THE DARK NIGHT OF THE SOUL
✧

"Last night I was gripped by the deep isolation that comes from living in a world that never seems kindred."
— *Carolyn Mary Kleefeld*

"I feel like a weary camper in another cycle, not sure exactly what this season of being /non-being will mean."
— *Carolyn Mary Kleefeld*

The "dark night of the soul", which many poets and artists struggle with in their lives, can owe some of its darkness to the at times unbearable aloneness of their vision and to their knowledge of "something more deeply interfused", their epiphanic experience of nature shining with the startling dew of eternity and the genuine belief that the Earth could—but for the madness of mankind—be Edenic. Also, there is the awareness of something forever beyond but out of one's touch, which American Theodore Roethke acknowledges: "The feeling that one is on the edge of many things: that there are many worlds from which we are separated by only a film."[1]

As the British academic and poet Robin Skelton has recognized, "What is a momentary depression or passing insecurity in the non-poet is for the poet a more serious matter; he will dwell upon it and live within it until he can, wracked by loss and despair, cry out with Milton's Samson Agonistes 'Dark, dark, dark amid the blaze of noon'.

Skelton goes on to say, "Dealing with such times of despair and aridity is not easy, but there are methods. The first, and obvious one, is to begin a poetic journal in which one can express one's state of mind".[2]

Carolyn expresses this sudden darkness across the light of the soul perfectly in a piece of writing from one of her unpublished works, *Rippling Revelations*, "I have temporarily become severed from my spiritual nature, from my core, from the miracle of the world, the Infinite."

Apart from the aloneness of her vision as a poet and an artist, Carolyn has her self-imposed solitary way of living, which can heighten a sense of "the dark night of the soul". As she writes in her book, *The Alchemy of Possibility*, "After all-consuming thrusts of energy, I find myself emptied, an opaque pool that can't reflect the heaven it once beheld." In the same book, she admits: "Feeling like an empty husk, I bend low to the ground, severed from my imagination. I have fallen from my heaven, my love-realm, with muddy wings, barely remembering the metabolism of Paradise" and "At times, I feel enslaved by the government of my mind. I tyrannize myself with endless tasks. Sometimes, when I am most fragile, I am the least kind to myself. The primitive animal within, driven by its own need to survive, preys on my vulnerabilities. I am both tyrant and slave, playing on my own cat-and-mouse games, capturing myself within self-made traps."

The need to escape is stressed time and again in her journal entries, "I need to leave here, to escape. The walls are moving in–even in this spacious paradisiacal land. Yet, there's nowhere truly for me to go. Just a few days, just a few different experiences and back I'll be like a rat in a treadmill, in the treadmill of my own making. Where is salvation? In art, love, friendship? Salvation has itself gone to sea, last seen gliding beyond the last horizon, obscured by its own nullity."

"The wind is worse, ruling paradise with a hellish ferocity. I must consider moving from here. One would never expect to be forced out of paradise, would one? But I feel I might be. The birds fly the currents in a frenzied call, swooping and soaring, will to the wind. The torrents of crazed air make me more restless, more scattered than ever."

On one of her many visits to Los Angeles, to see friends such as George and Peggy DiCaprio, father and stepmother of actor Leonardo, Carolyn asks herself: "Could I live here again? A place in the Hollywood Hills near where Laura Huxley lived? I could hike up in those mountains. What joy to be out of the wind."

She does, though, see the obvious differences between her Big Sur life and her Los Angeles 'life': "I return from an enriching gallop through Southern, CA with friends, back to the wind and solitary garden. Swallows dive the quivering blue currents. A hummingbird makes those clicking sounds near the lagoon as I swim. Many seagulls drift the ocean tides below. Everywhere and everything is blue today—the cobalt seas, the pastoral skies, the lingering mists. An airplane blasts its noise through the skies. The swallows dart and leap away from the cacophony. Ah, to fly like the swallow, diving, and soaring—such wondrous freedom their wings allow.

"The wind continues its rushing force through the forests, and the sea sings from its chains. Here, it is the elements, the land, forest, and seas. In LA, it is about people and museums, and human accomplishments, and the deadening, ceaseless traffic and dead cement. The city of the lost angels and glossy images—the slick city of human image, commodities sold as varnished products, a high-tech machine of digital people, honed in like a computer game.

Here the elements reign and the only overpopulation is the agapanthus in their blue and white bloom. A half-moon soars, looking marbleized and remote in the distant heavens.

"I spent the evening devouring the pile up of magazines. Tiring and mostly unrewarding. They yielded just an idea or two after three hours of mulling through. Everything appeared to be to get attention. I much enjoy the quietness. I feel as if I can sink into it and bathe. The LA world seems so far away now and so opposite. Also I see the total gaps here. I'm in between worlds. Not quite this, not quite that. How apropos to my nature. But the contrasts are quite necessary."

Unfinished Void by Carolyn Mary Kleefeld © 2010 Carolyn Mary KLeefeld
40" x 30" Acrylic and Oil on Canvas

It is these contradictions in her life, rural and occasionally urban, which also contribute to the energy of her creativity. The price of giving herself over to her muses can be heavy, "I'm particularly feeling my limits today and with that, a deep sorrow tugs at my soul. When I swoop into the dungeons, I forget that it's time again to examine the psyche's toxins. The strings of my Stradivarius instrument become so easily disturbed. The ecstasies and agonies of this kind of super sensitivity–the yellow canary again in the mines, discovering and suffering from these flights."

And: "I've fallen into a pit of reaction again. When will I ever learn? Or if one is as "morbidly sensitive"* as I, there is such repetition of theme that it's hard to bear, hard to accept one's eccentricities. [*D. H. Lawrence coined this description of a state of being.] There's a low-grade depression inhabiting me today, due to a variety of causes. Why don't I have the tools of not allowing these moods as others have? Because I loathe any kind of mechanics, I answer myself. Plus I can learn more by experiencing."

Her constant battle with her internal, ever-present and heightened sensitivity can even impact her desire and ability to create: "How can I possibly paint today, I'm so weary. I certainly identify with Herman Hesse and others on that most sensitive facet of being that decides what we can and cannot do."

"I certainly feel the isolation grip, without wheels and no chances of meeting people. I need to make things happen. (If they feel right, of course)."

There is, too, the eternal dilemma for the creative person, "Perhaps in grasping to explain life's meaning we dissipate its pulse."

If one creates, though, one must restart again and again from the uneasy silence of such depths. As the Irish poet W. B. Yeats declares:

> Now that my ladder's gone
> I must lie down where all the ladders start
> In the foul rag and bone shop of the heart."[3]

One must convince oneself in the moments of doubt of the specialness of what one is doing and offering. As Carolyn deliberates in one of her journal entries: "No,

I won't write another poem tonight, or even try to. Sometimes I just let the words come. No plan. No idea–as new, letting thought flow like the tides upon the shores. After all, how important should we make ourselves anyway, and who really cares if a poem is written tonight by me? Will it change the world? Will I help someone else? Wouldn't medical care or a hot meal help most problems more? Or is the spirit a dependent kind of energy that needs a rare pollen called poetry? And don't we need to nourish that indefinable spirit with the essences of feelings? Perhaps feelings and emotions need to be fed sometimes like starving entities roving through our hollow meadows . . .

"Yes, tonight the hollow night roared like a hungry beast growling for spiritual food, for the unseen. And when I finally let my pen travel the pages, the beast within finally laid down at my feet, satisfied at last."

Carolyn knows, as all creative people, she was born to create. The calling is in one's DNA and the emergence from a 'dark night of the soul' is itself an act of creation:

An Embryo Emerging

As an embryo emerging
from a grim winter,
she faces life anew.
The bedraggled forests lie flat
at her breaking root.

In a time wrought with anguish,
when the sun is denied
and the stars become infidels,
she is reborn.

Is this what it takes to be a poet?
Is this a madness
the gods confer upon the innocent?

The shy dawn is not ready
for this shrug of word.
Only the gauzy fog proclaims her,
protecting her embryo

from human gaze,
keeping her, for the moment,
in the eye of innocence—
the honesty of water.

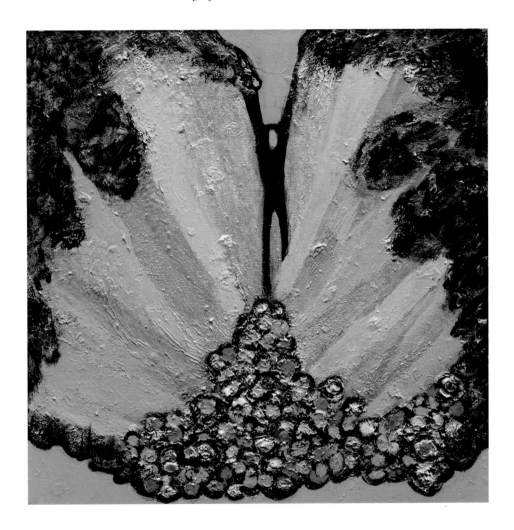

On the Abyss of Transformation by Carolyn Mary Kleefeld
© 2014 Carolyn Mary Kleefeld 20" x 20" Acrylic and Ink on Canvas

Chapter 11

THE SPIRIT OF THE PLACE

"I'm a vessel of the forces that be and I am humbled."
—Carolyn Mary Kleefeld

"I love being involved more with the wilderness that surrounds me. It inspires my paintings, my life, my soul to be in tune with Nature in such a way."
—Carolyn Mary Kleefeld

Carolyn has, time and time again, given the readers of her poetry and the viewers of her paintings the essence and the pulse of a particular place, indeed the spirit of the place. Her revealing of the startling dew of eternity diminishes any dark nights of her soul. As a writer and an artist, she will be forever synonymous with Big Sur. Like many of the great writers and artists, such as Wordsworth and Van Gogh, she has captured the spirit of a specific place: the genius loci. Time and again in her artwork and her writings, she reveals the landscape that surrounds her and its enduring undersong. Her journal entries over forty years are full of her reactions to multi-faced nature and the dramatic changes of the seasons. She is hypersensitive to the minutiae of her existence on a mountain that is constantly challenged by the sheer life-forces. The lack of people and properties on the mountain means that everything natural, untouched by man, is heightened, coloured more brightly, more sharply. Carolyn can observe as clearly and as purely as someone alone on an island.

She can let the symphony of different sounds, from the dragging roar of the nearby Pacific Ocean to the smallest of birds expressing its joy or its sorrow in its urgent tweets, seep into her very soul. Her chosen place is always offering up surprises, from the deliberate, majestic and visually ancient glide of a condor suddenly coming into sight to the frozen stare of a deer startled by the presence of an unexpected human.

Her journal entries are a literary treasure-trove of her observations: "I woke into another paradisiacal day, the sun's golden tresses heating the garden's bloom and transforming my ragged night's sleep into reconciliation. The dear little Oriole birds have made their nest already and their little chicks were chirping early this morning to my sleepless ears. It's another iridescent day, the sea–green and translucent seas with white dots of seagulls drifting. The fragrances of the heated flowers and buds thrill my senses, and the twitter of blooming birds fill my heart.

"I democratically save all [the] insects I can when swimming, from the tiny to the larger, ugly or not. And it pleases me in that delightfully simple way. The heavens are blue and pastoral like quiet and distant meadows. Hardly a cloud dare exist today. The day moves languorously forward."

She knows she is blessed to have her home in a world away from the "noisy sensation-impacted modern times": "How can I be so fortunate, I wonder, as I swim in my lagoon, sipping the pollen of this sun-kissed day, the flowers' scent rippling through my open senses. I'm quite sure I'm one of the last dinosaurs of these times. My senses are of another time. I depart this lagoon paradise above the ancient rolling sea, clucking to the crows that caw, carrying the budding flowers in bouquets to my soul. How did this happen, all this magic?"

In fact, the "magic" is the backdrop to her ever-unfolding growth as a creative woman. A writer since childhood, she *has* to turn what she observes around her and inside her into words. It is that internal giving oneself over to the demands of creativity that lead to the external wonders being captured. The poet, the writer, and the artist must cut off the irrelevant noise of life and totally focus on discovering the true music of being alive.

As she once wrote, "Every individual must stop long enough to listen to themselves."

The spirit of the place © 2018 Carolyn Mary Kleefeld Collection

Writing is in her very blood. "The storm appears to have fled and the satisfied white billowy clouds roam the skies, fleeting from their deliverance. And the deepened cobalt seas churn with the heaving storm of an anguish transfused, revivified, the mountain forests and gardens quelled with their heavenly feast. The tempests, chilling and fierce, rage like storm-gushing rivers through the forests, making my warm body recoil, thrashing and tearing like the savage barber of the trees' souls, making my warm body recoil.

I wondered when it would stop. The blue of the skies is reborn for the first time. This blue is born infused, reborn. Amorphic cloud images drift, changing at whim—free, careless as newborn infants in their glory. The incipient twilight sun floods through the trees, brightly glimmering like a dying diamond beckoning the icy wind to tear on. The mountains are illumined by the day's dying light. And the skies are like soft blue meadows, drifting in wonder, pastoral and forgiving.

"A condor lights on the pine tree quite near the pool. I cluck sounds to him. He opens his enormous wings. His head is vulture-like. I whistle my special sound to him and delight in his primordial presence. He fits so well in color and form with the dark green branches that I can't see him unless I'm at a certain vantage point."

"I came to the lagoon on this exceptionally calm day. I watched the night enshrouding the twilight and just before, two white herons flew over my head. I saw their dangling legs and exquisite white wings. I was in awe of their elegance. It seemed a lofty omen. Just now I saw a streak of light over the John Kaye mountain, a rivulet of fast traveling yellow light—another phenomenon of this sacred land."

Writing by hand, she brings her world to life via a concise and careful use of language.

"The white heron came again and this time I could see more of its exquisitry, its needle-like head and serpentine neck, divine whiteness of huge wings flopping as it perched in the dark green pine above the pool. What a thrill to see, behold its auspicious elegance.

"The fog has lifted its veils from the mountains, and the sea has lost its tidal striations. It's a quiet day along the coasterly views. The mist hugs the cliffs and diffuses the beaches with its mystical veils. The fog entities travel up the mountains again, obscuring the BB Nest, my remote cabin in the Ventana Hills, and blue skies. This misty day lends to my sense of vagary. [It] is soothing to bathe in the moistened, breezy air and the horizons are eclipsed in the billowy snow.

"The skies are filled with the clotted cream of white clouds assembled. A heat wave is finally here; [it's] in the 80's. A lizard, which may be pregnant, hovers above the lagoon and doesn't move when I touch it and lets ants run over it. I think it either is giving birth (large tummy) or dying. Well, we are all in these contrasts, whether oblivious to them or not.

"The white Shasta daisies are all shriveling in the heat, their spidery fingers, ragged and needy for water, or for death. The seas are quite calm. The patterns undulate in front of Edmund's, of beauty, of Nature's lyrics, of his continuing presence in my ghost life. The air is heavy with the ripened fragrances of these gardens above the sea. Alyssums and geraniums sweeten the ambrosia of scent.

"I gaze down into Edmund's sea gardens, imbibing the golden brown kelp drifting and the wavering music of the cobalt tides. Edmund and I were related in our passion for beauty. The splendor of this Mediterranean day— the Greek Isles are manifested in the blue oceanic lyrics of the tides below.

"I am stuck in the honey of this day, like a queen bee in her honeycomb of living.

"I hear the dry cackle of rippling eucalyptus leaves near me at the earthen crossroad where the friendly old wooden bench is perched with an infinite view of the awesome coastline. The skies are virgin blue and scarce with cloud. Shadows are coming to life in the approaching twilight. Hummingbirds throw lyrics from the eucalyptus boughs gilded in the sun's dying beams.

"It started to rain and gathered speed, with giant black clouds like seamless quilts covering the skies. It's been hailing madly, heav[il]y and consistently, as if the sky were falling into the earth with its winter burdens. It all seems far overdone, like it's out of balance and out of some tragedy of itself. It drowns us and the earth without a wink of light to offset its eccentric, relentless storming. When the sun scatters its light carelessly and frivolously, the air is so cold and windy, one can't go outside comfortably and enjoy a drop of the sunlight. The earth seems horridly out of whack, just like the humans. How can there be a separation anyway? Of course there's no difference, in a sense."

Time and again, she captures the essence of this sacred landscape, her artist's eye focused on the natural canvas: "Patricia came over and today was a superb day—totally obscured in the fog [but] gradually the sun was triumphant, breaking through the veils. It was phenomenal to see through the mists to the cobalt sea, through to the mountains. We hiked down the trail to Ithaca [her nickname for the beach below Edmund Kara's derelict cabin]. What deep pleasure to arrive in that 'untouched by humans' world. The tides were in and we received the negative ions galore. There we were, sitting on rocks as happy as could be! The waves were huge in places and like maverick occurrences, the lacy foam spuming from the waves, the wild terrain of sea. The subdued colors—sap green, gray, brown, black—and muddy waters. Earlier the aqua-blue waters were seen through the veils of mist.

"And then, after our commune on the rocks of the timeless, we began to ascend. By then the fog had returned and obscured it all. When we got to the top of the mountain, it all was erased by the opaque moisture, another truth revealed."

The night time view from her mountain-top home, always so impressive and magical, is profiled beautifully in this striking and compact poem:

Bursting With Secrets

Stray reflections vagrantly drift
across the twilight sea.

Drowsy mountains
dip rocky toes

into the singing sea,
growing black in

the cascading darkness.

And the harvest moon
threatens to burst with
all her silvery secrets,
letting them fall to earth
like love letters written
to our beseeching souls.

Within the spirit of her isolated place, she is always aware of the bigger picture, the world beyond: "What an ideal realm, this Ithaca is, untarnished by time, man and his thoughts. Just the migration of birds, the sun's diamonds sparkling in the undulating waters—the Mediterranean without the population explosion. I study the stones' color, eager to absorb the seminal, platonic colors. It's truly miraculous to realize that within every instant everything is going on—from the white egret lifting its wings to babies being born, to babies dying and murders of the innocent, people falling in love, people divorcing, planets being birthed, and planets dying. This bountiful cornucopia is impossible to comprehend fully in its vastness, its unlimited properties, and ingredients.

She has such a deep love for this landscape, " 'It's sheer magic,' I say to Patricia as we leave Ithaca, which reflects this infinite life. It's interesting that we are so drawn to this remote and primal shore by the sea covered in rocks. We hike up a kind of goat trail, as if we were peasants of Greece or any other indigenous people or natives of the Earth. Yes, we are drawn to the origins, to drink from the fountains of primal existence. Wildlife, animals, birds—all live this way, without seeking it, but they are not being asked to reveal consciousness. Edmund Kara lived that way, instinctively living the Tao."

The Wilds of Ithaca

(for Patricia)

A wild wind
races across the sea
like a cosmic conductor
orchestrating the tides
to rhapsodic lace.

We gaze in a trance
from our perch
at this tidal fugue
of white manes cresting
while coveys of gulls,
like musical notes,
drift on kelp beds
in the calm beyond.

And the cobalt sea glistens
from its wind-borne sheen
as it sweeps the rolling surf.

Carolyn at Ithaca, below her mountain-top home
© 2018 Carolyn Mary Kleefeld Collection

Her poetry and prose writings, for the most part, are accessible and direct and one can sense a specific landscape, her home on the 'Dragon's Crown' mountain, her very close proximity to the magnificent natural engine of the Pacific Ocean and the nearby ancient forest of redwoods. Her paintings, though, have often taken that specific landscape into incredible realms of the imagination, into the arena of the spiritual and the eternal, yet they are still pulsing with the life-force rhythms of her particular place. A fine example is her beautiful and inspired *Dream of Ithaca*.

As she says in her book *Visions from Big Sur*, "Art, like music, offers a language beyond words. To be innovative, it must be created from an inner wilderness, free of stale and redundant concepts."

Dream of Ithaca by Carolyn Mary Kleefeld
© 2005 Carolyn Mary Kleefeld 36" x 60" Acrylic and Ink on Canvas.

The artist at work © 2018 Peter Thabit Jones

Since settling in Big Sur in 1980, she has claimed her particular place, infusing it with a sense of eternity and often an aura of holiness. She has captured it in poems, writings, and paintings, and despite doing so for many decades, there is at the heart of her assured vision a refreshing innocence.

"Twilight tiptoes into the forests and across the sea—peaceful, graceful, yielding gradually to the night's ebony reign. This land of Atlantis casts its eternal spell and the full moon haunts the pulse of every breathing thing."

Chapter 12

THE CAROLYN CAMPAGNA KLEEFELD CONTEMPORARY ART MUSEUM
California State University Long Beach, California

✧

"Carolyn's impact on California art has been nothing short of remarkable and we are delighted that the University Art Museum will be part of her lasting legacy, as well as provide us with the opportunity to showcase her work and that of other notable artists,"
—California State University, Long Beach
President Jane Close Conoley

In February 2022, the California State University Long Beach opened the Carolyn Campagna Kleefeld Contemporary Art Museum. The redesigned and expanded museum includes a diverse selection of Carolyn's artwork, along with her literary archives, journals and manuscripts.

The Carolyn Campagna Kleefeld Contemporary Art Museum shortly after its completion in early 2022 © 2022 Georgia Freedman-Harvey

The museum held a "Celebration of the Arts" on 20th May 2022 to welcome invited guests. This marked the formal reopening of the museum and a milestone in the history of the museum. Guests could view the museum and see the five inaugural exhibitions, including an exhibition highlighting Carolyn's artwork called *In-Between the Silence: Carolyn Campagna Kleefeld.*

Carolyn's donation made it possible to expand and renovate the former University Art Museum. The gift created the opportunity for the museum to achieve its long-time goals and visions for the collection and for better serving the community. Through Carolyn's generosity, the museum can actively build on the size and breath of the collection and offer a state-of-the-art venue that encourages advancement of scholarly research by the CSULB faculty and art scholars. The museum adheres to the standards established by the American Alliance of Museums, of which it is an accredited member. Carolyn's donation allowed for an additional 4,000 square feet plus to be added to the existing space, and a reconfiguring of the entire museum to provide a model museum teaching facility on the University campus. The new space includes dedicated collection storage, an archival and reading room, education room, and gallery space dedicated to special exhibitions, a project exhibit space that allows for viewing of videos and other experimental artworks, and a gallery space dedicated to sharing Carolyn's artwork.

For the first time the museum has its own HVAC and internal security system. The newly built education laboratory is at the core of the museum mission and will be a place to provide hands-on learning materials for university students, youths, and adults. For the first time, the entire museum collection will be housed on campus, including the prestigious "Hampton Collection". By having the collection stored in one place, the museum can expand its exhibition offerings focused on the collection and provide expanded access to researchers and other museums to utilize all aspects of this very rich and diverse collection.

The building received a LEED Silver building sustainability rating and includes solar panels on the roof. This designation brings prestige to the museum and CSULB. A spacious outdoor garden, decorated with native and water-wise plants surrounds new outdoor seating areas, and allows for outdoor performances and places for the University community to gather.

The new addition also includes generous office spaces, a visitor's lobby and reception area, a retail shop to highlight the artwork of CSULB alumni, a community gallery, and easier access into the museum, giving more visibility on the CSULB campus. This was a key factor in the design to make the museum more inviting and encouraging for students to feel welcome in the space. The museum is also fully accessible.

One of the designated collection storage spaces has been named the David Campagna Prints and Drawings Room, which houses the museum's impressive collection of prints, drawings, and works on paper—including those by Lee Krasner, Robert Rauschenberg and others—and Carolyn's works on paper. This room will be accessible by appointment. Researchers and faculty are encouraged to use the collection to expand their research and/or hold classes in the space.

Carolyn's gift to CSULB goes beyond the walls of the museum and was designed to expand the reach of the museum on the campus through the ongoing support of a multi-disciplinary lecture series, art scholarships for the College of the Arts (COTA), staff interns, and an endowment to help insure the long-term viability of the museum and the arts at CSULB. Her gift speaks to the mission of the University through meeting its goal of providing "educational opportunities through superior teaching, research, creative activity, and service for the people of California and the world."

Carolyn's gift has been viewed as a "game changer" for CSULB and the surrounding communities. The impact of the gift is best expressed by university President Jane Close Conoley, Cyrus Parker-Jeannette, who is the former Dean of the College of the Arts, and is now Dean Emeritus, and Paul Baker Prindle, the Director of the museum. "The expanded museum provides CSULB with unique scholarship, innovation, and service opportunities," said President Jane Close Conoley. "The new expansion allows for greater levels of engagement with the diverse communities we serve, and our hope is to make it available to as many groups as possible. Further, we are delighted that this 'laboratory for cultural exploration' is housed in a facility that showcases [CSULB's] commitment to sustainability." The university President also stated, "Our entire campus community, as well as our surrounding communities and the art world at-large will benefit as a result of Ms. Kleefeld's extraordinary generosity and foresight."

Cyrus Parker-Jeannette said, "Our goal at the University Art Museum is to promote a nuanced interpretation of museum exhibitions and collections and provide an opportunity for students and the public to deepen their understanding of the complex role art plays in culture. Ms. Kleefeld's exemplary gift provides us with the ability to exceed that goal. It will allow us to highlight her career and impact, better share the work of extraordinary artists, and expose our communities to important and powerful works. As I reflect on the impact of this gift, I am struck by this anonymous quote, 'When courage, genius and generosity hold hands, all things are possible'. The generosity of Carolyn Campagna Kleefeld's gift, both of her art and financial support provided, is a game changer for our museum. It is transformational for the future and spirit of our exhibits and will inevitably deepen the experience for our students, faculty, community and scholars who visit."

The Carolyn Campagna Kleefeld Museum, of course, is also open to the world, via the internet and all the resources that the online world offers.

Paul Baker Prindle, the current museum director, joined the team as construction was about to begin and has been a key player in seeing the building though to completion, and the reopening of the new space. The director, along with the staff, worked to create a welcoming environment that reflects on the core mission of the museum to create a community of people who examine, critique, create, and enjoy contemporary art and culture.

Paul Baker Prindle summed up the transformation by saying "After two years of working to expand and transform our museum, we are overjoyed to welcome our communities to experience our arts complex, new exhibitions and more. We are very excited to advance our focus on visual abstraction, material innovation and arts integration and offer improved access to our collection as an educational resource that is owned by all Californians."

Carolyn views the museum as an example of her commitment to the importance of supporting and inspiring creativity, and as an achievement in her life as an artist and poet, which ensures a lasting legacy for her decades of dedicated creative expression, and stated, "A profound circle has magically manifested. When my parents, S. Mark and Amelia Taper, came to this country from England with my brother, sister, and myself, we first stayed for some time at the Biltmore Hotel in

Long Beach, and later my father began his extensive housing for veterans there. So, now for my life's work to be part of the Long Beach community is a destiny fulfilled, a circle of fate completed.

As I express in my artist statement, 'ultimately art is an innocent interactive mirror of my innermost process, whisking me out of time into the Timeless. My life's passion is to create art from this unconditioned well of being and to inspire such a journey in others.' Thus, to have my art and writing in this educational setting is a dream realized, and my aspiration is for the students and visitors to the university to embark on their own journeys of inner discovery and creative expression, inspired by my own experiential explorations."

PLATE 3

13. Paul Baker Prindle, Director of the Museum, Carolyn, Tiger Windwalker, Patricia Holt, and Georgia Freedman-Harvey at Carolyn's home
© 2022 Dale Diesel

14. President Jane Close Conoley giving a welcoming address at the event on 20th May 2022 © 2022 Tiger Windwalker

15. Carolyn with her 'Love-Muse' Arthur Williamson at the 20th May event
© 2022 George DiCaprio

16. George DiCaprio, environmentalist and father of Leonardo, Arthur,
Carolyn, and Tiger Windwalker at the 20th May event
© 2022 Peggy DiCaprio

17. General festivities at the event on 20th May 2022
© 2022 Evan Landy

18. Carolyn, Carolyn's personal assistant and dear friend Laura Zabrowski
and her husband Frank at the 20th May event
© 2022 Gilberto Valencia

19. Some of Carolyn's paintings in Carolyn's Gallery
© 2022 Georgia Freedman-Harvey

20. Carolyn's painting, *Fertile Entity* and her Donor Statement in the main lobby © 2022 Georgia Freedman-Harvey

21. The state-of-the-art education room © 2022 Georgia Freedman-Harvey

22. David Campagna Prints and Drawings Room
© 2022 Georgia Freedman-Harvey

23. The Reading and Archive Room
© 2022 Georgia Freedman-Harvey

Interestingly, during the construction of the museum, an evergreen tree was placed on the beam to signify construction has reached the sky. It also symbolizes positive things: good luck for future occupants, new or continued growth in concert with the environment, and a safe job, well done.

The tree is an ancient construction tradition. There are many such rites associated with a new edifice including the laying of foundation stones, the signing of beams, and ribbon-cuttings. But what's particularly charming about the construction tree is that it isn't associated with the beginning or the end of construction. Rather, the tree is associated with the raising of a building's highest beam or structural element. Hence the name of the rite: the "topping-out" ceremony. It's a sign that a construction project has reached its literal apogee, its most auspicious point. The tree is now planted at Carolyn's home, to continue to grow and flourish.

The evergreen tree placed on the signed beam
© 2022 Georgia Freedman-Harvey

The signing of the beam
© 2022 Georgia Freedman-Harvey

This museum is a fitting legacy to Carolyn's artistic, and, indeed, her poetic life. She has followed the paths of her creative vision determinedly through the years. The blank canvas and the blank page have been her calling. It is also a genuine joy for all those who are aware of and admire Carolyn's indefatigable vision in her approach to the act of creation.

The fact that Carolyn's generous gift to the university will assure a dynamic, unique educational experience for the students and California State University Long Beach community means The Carolyn Campagna Kleefeld Museum will fulfil Carolyn's desire to encourage creativity as a way of life in others. Also, in this world of technology, people internationally will be able to partake and experience the Museum via the internet.

To turn Carolyn's generosity into reality, to achieve and see to completion this remarkable project, it took a group of dedicated and talented people. Carolyn says:

" I am thankful beyond measure to Patricia's dedication and talents to making this happen, and to Georgia Freedman-Harvey, curator, art consultant and colleague with Patricia in this museum project, who has such focus of vision and devotion. Also, to Kirtana who through the years has kept me going, recorded all of my work digitally—ensured I am inspired and able to continue." This is an extraordinary success for Carolyn and her partners, Patricia Holt, and Kirtana. The project will have a lasting impact on furthering artistic conversations.

As a species on this ever-changing planet, with the extreme challenges we face in this century, we need creativity. We need to sow the seeds of future artists and writers in the coming new generations of young people and in those older people who are seeking a more spiritual and rewarding aspect to their busy lives. The Carolyn Campagna Kleefeld Contemporary Art Museum is a truly inspiring contribution to such a vision.

Afterword

"Anyway, where else does our art come from but the experiences of our lives?"
—*Carolyn Mary Kleefeld*

"You have no idea of your creative genius, reverential pleaching of worlds, yet always the human caress in voice and vision." —Vince Clemente, New York emeritus professor of English, poet, critic, and editor, written to Carolyn, from his Introduction to her book Psyche of Mirrors[1]

Carolyn Mary Kleefeld's life is a wonderful example of a life given over wholeheartedly to the creative act, to prose, to art and to poetry. The rudder of all of her writings and all of her paintings is a realization that the personal is fused to the universal and that the universal is fused to the personal; and that nature is the revelation of holiness, the picturesque and the uncaring rage of its life-forces. As the American writer and critic and New York emeritus professor Vince Clemente has intimated, Carolyn Mary Kleefeld has a Wordsworthian commitment to being the solitary observer.

Her works, poetry and paintings, are honest and poetic, inspired and inspiring, lyrical and visual, and they give us insights into a variety of subjects. We get the inner wilderness and the outer wilderness of an independent-thinking woman.

She can word-paint the minutiae and the panoramic of the Big Sur landscape. It is an original and very individual voice, sometimes very strong and sometimes very vulnerable. One always senses in the works, to paraphrase the English poet Edward Thomas, the artist's and the poet's frustration of not being able to 'bite the day to the core', to get beyond the so-called 'real'. That said, we also get in her work what another English poet Thom Gunn, who settled in California, called 'a sniff of the real'.

One also senses the personal philosophy of someone who has seen through the flesh to the bone of contemporary life, and yet there can still be an innocent child-like wonder when confronted with aspects of the natural world. She is tuned into the music of the natural world, its seasons, its symphonies of light throughout the day and the night, and the rhythmic pulses of her art; poetry and prose come out of that music. She has succeeded in establishing a formidable creative voice, a voice and creativity denied to many of her female ancestors; and her knowledge of that historical familial fact is part of the energy and the passion of her works.

She is a poet and an artist visiting and revisiting, constantly contemplating and capturing, certain things that intrigue her. Her life is devoted to wondering about, exploring and searching for the essence of some 'truth'. As she has noted, "The explorers write outside of history, because to be an experimenter requires the willingness to ride the wave of the instant, to let oneself be carried to the ever-expanding shores of verdant awareness."

She has said of her writing process, "I need the shape, form, sound and meaning of words to ripple through my veins like blood-music, dripping through me, my pen, madly; and I frantically try to capture the words as they spill out like geysers from a deeper place within. Out of the roots of me, the words grow through the alchemy of my ingredients and then appear, in spite of me, congratulating me, if I don't get in their way, a kind of respect for my making myself quite invisible and merely being a desperately devoted slave to the pen's music. Am I conducting? Do I create the art? The words? The images? It's more like we create each other. I am an instrument of the unseen."

And she has declared when it comes to her process of painting, "I also let the paintings take me where they need to go. They are teaching me, as interactive media, straight from the Book of Life. They are pulsing, palpable creations, molecular entities escaping from my rib-caged, physical self, expressing as dutiful, loving, wise children what I need to do to improve them, to so-called *finish* them. Just the compulsion to finish them has taught me that seldom does that word have true meaning. It's more likely that nothing is ever finished; it's just a matter of how long you can stay engaged. And as these entities take me through their development of palpable, spiritual, visual manifestation, they speak silently and symbolically of my philosophies, introducing new insights and reaffirming the established ones. It's an interactive, inner-active education, filled with discovery and exploration. The paintings also, as in life, become most demanding in their last stages, growing their pinky nails that need polish and other last minute edges. This is where my patience, endurance, and lower back go through the most challenge. But somehow my need to create from the heathen caves of existence keeps echoing and asking for further development and refinement, teaching me to see more, both inwardly and of the so-called *real* world."

As the writer, editor, and Carolyn's beloved friend David Jay Brown stresses in his Commentary to Carolyn's *Songs of Ecstasy* book: "Not since William Blake has an artist so brilliantly captured the realm of ecstatic vision as Carolyn Kleefeld has, and she is the first, to my mind to do it from a feminine perspective."[2]

Dr. Timothy Leary, one of the twentieth century's iconic cultural figures, says in the same book, "Her wonderful writing moved me in all ways at once. . . She performs a rare literary alchemy, fusing science and sensuality, genetics and generosity, global biology and personal biography, high humour and profound insight, the microscopic detail of this moment with the grand sweep of evolution."[3] Carolyn was his favourite painter and her art is on the back cover of one of his books.

One can only admire the decades of creative output, the total devotion to the page and the canvas, and the cohesive aspect of all she produces. It is an astonishing achievement, given her early privileged life, when she could have chosen to go down a very different road. That she chose the road to poetry and art is her readers' and viewers' gain. All those who have commented on her works down the years, such as Dr. Timothy Leary, Dr. Carl A. Faber, Laura Archera Huxley, Stanislav Grof, Terence McKenna, Chungliang Al Huang, Dr. John C. Lilly, David Jay Brown, and Vince Clemente, were so right to recognize a prodigious and remarkable talent.

She has followed the paths of her creative vision determinedly through the years. The blank canvas and the blank page have been her calling. Her journey has been the exploration of the fathomless tides of the heart.

Here is a journal entry that Carolyn wrote in 2015, when I started my journey in trying to capture some of the essence and some of the aspects of her fascinating life. It was yet another summer for my annual writer's residency in her cabin in Big Sur. She wrote, "I dragged the black bag of manuscripts, a great metaphor, down to Peter's cabin—thump, thump, thump over the cobblestones—the black bag of my life, manuscripts going back to 1988." For me, that "black bag of my life" was a gift full of treasures.

Carolyn Mary Kleefeld, poet and artist
Photo: John Larson © Carolyn Mary Kleefeld Collection

Notes

Chapter 1

1. Interview with David Jay Brown and Rebecca Ann Hill in *Women of Visionary Art*, edited by David jay Brown and Rebecca Ann Hill.
2. From William Wordsworth's "Lines composed a few miles above Tintern Abbey", *The Collected Poems of William Wordsworth*.
3. Vince Clemente's Introduction to Carolyn's book *Psyche of Mirrors: A Promenade of Portraits*.

Chapter 4

1. From Dylan Thomas's poem "The force that through the green fuse drives the flower", *Collected Poems* by Dylan Thomas.
2. From W. H. Auden's poem "In Memory of W. B. Yeats", *Collected Poems* by W. H. Auden.

Chapter 5

1. From *Big Sur and the Oranges of Hieronymus Bosch* by Henry Miller.
2. Interview with David Jay Brown in *Mavericks of the Mind: Conversations for the New Millennium*, edited by David Jay Brown and Rebecca McClen Novick.
3. Interview with David Jay Brown in *Mavericks of the Mind: Conversations for the New Millennium*, edited by David Jay Brown and Rebecca McClen Novick.
4. Interview with David Jay Brown and Rebecca Ann Hill in *Women of Visionary Art*, edited by David jay Brown and Rebecca Ann Hill.
5. From Michael Zakian's Introduction to the 2008 Exhibition Catalog, *Retrospective: Carolyn Mary Kleefeld/Visions of Big Sur*.
6. Interview with David Jay Brown and Rebecca Ann Hill in *Women of Visionary Art*, edited by David jay Brown and Rebecca Ann Hill.
7. Interview with David Jay Brown and Rebecca Ann Hill in *Women of Visionary Art*, edited by David Jay Brown and Rebecca Ann Hill.
8. Interview with David Jay Brown and Rebecca Ann Hill in *Women of Visionary Art*, edited by David jay Brown and Rebecca Ann Hill
9. From W. B. Yeats's *The Collected Works in Verse and Prose of William Butler Yeats*.
10. From W. B. Yeats's poem "All things can tempt me from this craft of verse", *The Poems Collected Works of W. B. Yeats*.

Chapter 6

1. From Edward Thomas's poem "I never saw that land before", *Collected Poems* by Edward Thomas.

Chapter 7

1. Interview with David Jay Brown and Rebecca Ann Hill in *Women of Visionary Art*, edited by David Jay Brown and Rebecca Ann Hill.

Chapter 8

1. David Campagna interviewed by John Dotson in *The Seventh Quarry Swansea*
2. *Poetry Magazine*/David Campagna Special Supplement Summer Issue (2016).
3. David Campagna interviewed by Eleni Economides in *East Bay Times*/18th October 2006.
4. Interview with David Jay Brown and Rebecca Ann Hill in *Women of Visionary Art*, edited by David jay Brown and Rebecca Ann Hill.
5. David Campagna interviewed by John Dotson in *The Seventh Quarry Swansea Poetry Magazine*/David Campagna Special Supplement Summer Issue (2016).

Chapter 10

1. From David Wagoner (ed.), *Straw for the Fire: from the Notebooks of Theodore Roethke*, edited by David Wagoner.
2. Robin Skelton in *The Practice of Poetry*.
3. From W. B. Yeats's poem "The Circus Animals' Desertion", *The Poems Collected Works of W. B. Yeats*.

Afterword

1. Vince Clemente's Introduction to Carolyn's book *Psyche of Mirrors: A Promenade of Portraits*.
2. From David Brown's Commentary in Carolyn's book *Songs of Ecstasy*.
3. Dr. Timothy Leary in Carolyn's book *Songs of Ecstasy*.

Index

Carolyn Mary Kleefeld © Carolyn Mary Kleefeld Collection